THE GORELETS OMNIBUS

Collected Poems, 2001-2011

Paperback Edition

Michael A. Arnzen

Acclaim for *Gorelets*

"Bored with sleeping? Read this book at night. Michael Arnzen's poems are absolutely terrifying. His writing makes me uncomfortable for all the right reasons. If you enjoy the things that go bump in the night, Arnzen's poems might change your mind. Arnzen is disturbingly, madly, brilliant and I pray for those close to him." —Ryan Mecum, author of *Zombie Haiku* and *Dawn of Zombie Haiku*

"Horror and poetry very rarely mix well—if at all—but with *Gorelets*, Michael Arnzen has produced something of minor miracle; not only does every piece in this marvelous collection stand up to the rules applicable to poetry, but each piece—like the best horror story—provides the reader with chills—no small feat. If, on occasion, Mr. Arnzen's tongue is obviously pushed toward his cheek, it's all in fun—albeit intelligent, well-crafted fun. These pieces, and this collection, will not disappoint." —Gary A. Braunbeck

"SCARY. Achieves in your face, punching rhythmical effects. Coupled with Arnzen's vivid visuals...these rhythms are confrontational, leaving readers no place to run and hide." —*Sidereality*

"Tight and succinct...visionary fragments, sharp little pictures that make your stomach squirm...in regular English, avoiding the pretense that consume so many other poets." —Feomante.com

"Like one of those stubborn and painful scabs, only Arnzen could pull this one off. Served up with humor both vitreous and gut-wrenching, *Gorelets* delivers its tasty mind-morsels in palatable portions both raw and rare. If you haven't tried one yet, grab a plate and dig in." —Kurt Newton

THE GORELETS OMNIBUS, COLLECTED POEMS, 2001-2011

This edition commemorates the 10th anniversary of the original poetry series published via http://www.gorelets.com. The first book version, *Gorelets: Unpleasant Poems* was published by Fairwood Press in 2003. An expanded ebook edition was simultaneously published in electronic form by Double Dragon Ebooks in 2003. An extended publishing history appears in the appendices of this book, and should be considered an extension of this copyright page.

Published by Raw Dog Screaming Press
Bowie, MD

First Edition

Cover Image "Scaredy Cat" by Michael Arnzen
Cover & Book Design by Jennifer Barnes

Printed in the United States of America

ISBN 978-1-935738-21-3

Library of Congress Control Number: 2011945261

www.RawDogScreaming.com

Dedicated...

to

The Patron Saints

&

for

Millicent Frastley

Gratitude to...

Ryan Michael Williams introduced me to handheld computing and started all this. Kurt Newton supported this project with much gusto, as did Peggy Shumate, Rebecca Baker, Bruce Siskawicz, and all the many patrons. Jacob Weisman helped me commit to a domain name. Patrick & Honna Swenson brought the electrons to the page. Deron Douglas indulged me with some extra electrons. Renate rubbed my back and smiled. Larry Connolly, Dave Sandner, and Gina Wisker generously shared their scholarship. Jennifer Barnes and John Edward Lawson continue to indulge me and voraciously bark alongside me. I thank all of you, and every single reader who ever carried these words in their pockets or their minds.

CONTENTS

What Are Gorelets?
An Introduction by Michael Arnzen

"Gorelets" is a neologism—a word I made up—for the little gory things I sometimes write that might otherwise be called "short-short horror poems." But I like to imagine there's a unique logic and structure to them; a specific "type" of horror poem that typifies the "gorelet"…mostly because they were *composed* in a manner that I believe uniquely shaped them.

In its initial incarnation in 2001, gorelets.com was the home of my weekly series of horror poems, called, "Gorelets: Unpleasant Poetry." The series was an experiment in delivery and form, as the poems were all written on—and designed to be read upon—the first handheld/mobile computers—"Palm Pilots" and "Handspring Visors" (yesterday's iPhones and BlackBerries). I self-published these once a week for a full year as a creative challenge.

Why? I received a PDA (which stands for "personal digital assistant") as a gift, and since I wasn't a corporate suit, I didn't know what else to do with it, so I used it as a literary toy instead. Luckily, I found others out there who were playfully adopting the devices as something more than just a way to keep appointments, and those readers were curious about what weirdness I could come up with next to desecrate their pristine technology. Maybe it made the devices a little more personal and human, somehow. Horror fans could subscribe to the service whether they owned a PDA or not, as, for a small fee, they were given access to a private online archive. Collectible postcard versions with original mail art were also released weekly to patrons who donated cash to support the development of the project, whose initial goal was to bring attention to poetry in the growing e-book community, as well as providing me with a creative playground for exploring new forms for shaping an experience of horror.

Looking back on the project now, ten years later, I see how widespread these kinds of literary games and self-publishing experiments have become. Nowadays, everyone's probably heard about "cell phone novels" and many a creative writer has exploited the new media challenges of twitter, facebook, wikis, iPhone apps, and much, much more. I find all these formats exciting, because I have always been a believer in McLuhan's classic expression, "the medium is the message." Most of the media we find online and in mobile technology are intended for information gathering or information management, and—with the exception of some apps for the ipad or android tablets—seem less interested in creativity as they are interested in selling us things that others create. I prefer to mess around with these things in ways they aren't intended to be used, to see what new forms of horror they might harbor. I also enjoy the liberty that indie publishing brings to the table, because it allows writers like me to be as weird as we wanna be. But at the time I first conceived of this idea, I was sort of making it all up as I went along, treating the work as a personal challenge to keep writing poetry on a weekly basis. Not many others were doing anything similar at the time, and ebooks were only starting to seem like a viable format because very few readers had the devices.

So Gorelets was sort of a little sideshow I was doing to stimulate my creative juices. It wasn't so much a publicity stunt as a self-imposed instigation for me to generate a live, serial poetry chapbook.

Poems, I felt, were the perfect content for the small screen size and portability of the handheld computer (and still are, I feel, for ebook reading devices). But, bafflingly, there was—and continues to be—a lack of poetry, let alone genre-oriented poetry, available in that format. Gorelets was an attempt to correct that, by not only providing short poetry for those who wanted to read it, but also by following a strict rule: to pack as much meaning into one single screen on the device as possible. This explains the "-lets" suffix, since in my mind these poems were akin to computer "applets" (mini-applications, or "apps" as they say in Apple land). Little applications of gore.

The project was personal, but it became public fast and having a steady set of subscribers really encouraged me to be disciplined and timely with the one-poem-per-week rule. I tracked a goodly number of hits on the webpage, and the number of readers increased with every release as word of mouth spread. The site eventually received press coverage in venues ranging from *Wired* magazine to *Pittsburgh City Paper* to *Jobs In Hell* and I even got calls for several radio interviews. You might think that such coverage is expected for a horror writer, and that publicity is just part of the job. And you'd be right in most cases. But it was remarkable for poetry to get attention like this. The emotional support of such validation and the great reactions from readers (who would email me their gut reactions and eagerness for the next piece) was really encouraging, emotionally. And I also was encouraged by the financial contributions of loyal readers. I worked on a "patronage" system (not unlike today's kickstarter) and, overall, the project received enough donations from readers to fund its entire production, and the 52 poem series met its goal of launching a poem a week from August 2001 to August 2002.

A year after the project ended, the poems were printed in a collectable chapbook by Fairwood Press in a unique, fat, pocket-sized chapbook, along with a special lettered edition. In addition to poetry, it included the artwork I'd designed on the computer to use for the "postcard" edition of the poems that went to patrons. Double Dragon Press at the same time also published a special e-book edition (long before Kindles were invented) which featured 21 bonus poems.

The project earned recommendations for the Bram Stoker Award in Alternative Forms...and the Fairwood Press edition was a finalist for the Poetry award. The book, moreover, has been taught in several horror fiction-oriented college classrooms, alongside my collection of flash fiction, *100 Jolts: Shockingly Short Stories* (Raw Dog Screaming Press, 2004)—and several of the poems were even adapted into a film (*Exquisite Corpse*, directed by Jim Minton in 2006). These minimalist works have been the subject of several academic studies, such as the panel on "Michael Arnzen's New Directions in Horror" from the International Conference for the Fantastic in the Arts in 2006, which resulted in several papers printed in *Dissections: The Journal of Contemporary Horror* (these papers are reprinted in this book, and I'll try not to say much more about the history of the project now, since Lawrence C.

Connolly's essay does a much better job of recounting the history of this in relation to the genre than I ever could).

For a year's worth of tapping out creepy ideas on a silly electronic device, the Gorelets series truly exceeded my expectations!

But even though I feel the "experiment" was a success, it was so much fun that I couldn't just stop when I hit poem #52 poem after that first year. So I created an electronic newsletter to continue the project, with the benefit of no longer being constrained by the handheld computer or restricted by weekly time commitments. I called it "The Goreletter," and several of the strange short writings that appeared in it—or on the new weblog edition of it—appear in this grand "Omnibus" edition of the Gorelets project.

In fact, the Goreletter continues to this very day, and I earnestly invite you to subscribe at: http://www.gorelets.com

To my glee, The Goreletter won the Bram Stoker Award in 2003 in a category the Horror Writers Association called "Alternative Forms." This category for the award no longer exists (and I have included my acceptance speech elsewhere in this omnibus for the curious). I was humbled by this accolade, but I also felt it reflected the growing interest in electronic publishing at the time—something which by today has skyrocketed to such proportions that amazon.com reports selling more ebooks than print books anymore.

But more than just "growing interest" exists in electronic publishing and this is more than just a curious social trend for me. If "the medium is the message" then, for writers, the electronic media requires a rethinking of how the medium *shapes* the message they are creating. How does the form of horror change its content? Doesn't a film version of a novel—even one directed and controlled by the author—work differently than the novel itself? Don't writers exploit the technology of the printed page as much as they do the language they employ, in order to generate "page-turners"? Don't poets play with the "negative space" in page layout to give shape and structure to their pensive musings?

What I mean by all these questions, is that I believe electronic formats should not merely be "adaptations" that transfer a story from print to electronic form. I think that they offer up shapes and structures and delivery pathways to the brain that are yet to be discovered, and writers absolutely should exploit the potentialities for new experiences (in the case of horror fiction, dread and terror). I am not so full of myself to suggest that Gorelets really accomplishes much new in this regard, but I do hope readers will keep in mind that there would be no gorelets without the device on which they were written, which seriously limited what I could and couldn't do on the "page."

As I suggested in my acceptance speech for the Stoker Award in "Alternative Forms," I believe that horror writing is itself an alternative form in the literary marketplace. I see the horror genre as an experimental playground for exploring the dark side of self and society; and sometimes you have to get into this abnormal territory by taking abnormal steps. Gorelets are but one alternative means toward the same end as a Stephen King novel or a Bentley Little story or a Wes Craven film or an iD computer game. But they are short, meant to be taken in tiny doses. I have collected these abnormal poems here as not merely a record of my experiment, but as an alternative means for readers to think abnormally about things—if only during a stolen snippet of time.

Thanks for indulging me with this "Omnibus" edition which includes everything horror poetry-related I have written over the past decade for the Gorelets.com website. Some readers may be wondering "why should I read this when I can read it all online?" but believe me, you can't. *The Gorelets Omnibus* is packed with material, some new, some unattainable, some only the most diehard of Arnzen fans would probably have seen. It includes the original *Gorelets* chapbook in its entirety, everything that also was included in the "extended" edition ebook, and everything I've ever published in *The Goreletter* under the "Gorelets" heading. It also includes a wide variety of pieces that have appeared on my website—from little side projects that only those who have burrowed around on the web have discovered to poems that were splashed briefly onto the internet but eventually were taken down and are no longer available online and impossible to find elsewhere. Those who buy the hardcover edition of this collection will get even more bonus features, like the hard-to-find Martha Stewart parody, *Michael Arnzen Dying*, originally published by Tachyon Publicaitons, all the haiku I've written that

I could find, and in the vein of DVD extras, I've even tossed in poems that I wrote on my PDA during the first year of the project that I never sent out to readers or publishers; these are merely drafts and I deemed them not as good as those that were used for the chapbook. The hardcover also has a lengthy "horror poetry writing workshop" that features essays on the genre and the entire collection of "Instigation" (creative writing prompts on the dark side) from The Goreletter. What's an Omnibus for, if not "everything" (*omni-*) archived (*-bus*)? So for kicks, I've added a sampler of other things I've self-published online that you may not have seen, from humorous "lists" from *The Goreletter* to poems I've been posting intermittently to twitter for about three years now (you can follow me at http://twitter.com/MikeArnzen).

In many ways, I feel like twitter provides a field of play that has come full circle from the Gorelets project I started a decade ago, and I love to read other writers' short horror poetry as it pops on my screen for a brief encounter before scrolling away and moving on to the next one.

Some say these twitter-like approaches to writing are symptomatic of a multitasking "snack culture" society that no longer is able to concentrate on any one thing for more than a flicker of time. Some might go so far as to interpret these poems as fragmented signs of a postmodern culture where no one is connected anymore in a genuine way. Sure we're evolving, or maybe devolving, but who's ever to really know the ultimate significance of any text in the first place? Maybe there's some horror lurking in the disconnection inherent to our touch-and-go society—some sense of infection in the "touch," some uncanny presence lurking along with us when we "go." I would say we are haunted more than fragmented by our awareness of the temporary nature of our own existence, and words have always been a way of marking time. Here's a book-length marker. I hope you find something creepy enough in here to stick to your ribs.

—Michael Arnzen, Halloween 2011

UNPLEASANT POEMS

The Original Gorelets (2001-2)

Nails

grip my thumb tightly
in your carpenter's pinch
and press the moonsliver ridge
against the score in the wood.
my denuded knuckle—
a fitting hook on this sick
pegboard of people and parts—
and strong enough to hold
the hammer you're swinging.

Worm

Naked in soil
Writhing red wet and blind
Puckering tip and tapering tail,
I wonder if there's any of you
Left in its belly
As I bring down the shovel
On your collarbone
Splitting you both in two

Brain Chunks

always locked
inside a box
of bone—it's
rather unctuous

always soft
as tofu quiche
but never quite
as scrumptious

grenemean

bonesnap
brittlecrack
splintergrizzle
numb

slurpsmack
crungiefungie
tricklepus
yum

Velcro

You hook me up
to a machine of wire—
a thousand piercings per inch—
and slip me out
of this pale costume
only to stick me
to you.

Petfood Breakfast

there's cat in my coffee
dog in my drink
a grinding machine
in my kitchen sink
hair on the counter
hair on the floor
but no hair at all
on my rare pet's paws
well
'cept those in the slaw

Zombeanie Babies

The tiny rhino's eyes gleam grey
as the featherless toucan swings
on the baby giraffe's upturned head,
dangling down his erect broken neck.
Happy monkey scratches his ribs,
satanically squeals, and spills his guts
as the dead kitten purrs wetly
beside the stiff boa at your ankles.
They've come to collect you.

Sonogram Surprise

Beneath the smeared lube
a rhythm kicks an offbeat tempo
as you watch an ultrasonic
red white and black miasma
firm into a hazy hand a heavy head
a kernel of open eye, watching
cautious as you clutch your chest
because you only came here
to unclog your laboring heart.

Open Casket Upholstery

There's not enough satin
under her skin.
Not enough stuffing,
her pillow's too thin.
This stitching's atrocious—
they call this embalmed?
I'll fill them wrong, too,
once my nerves have calmed.

Sunk

squalid skull
spurts silt snot—
sunken sailor
once sneezed
seeking safer
sand

Collarbone Custard

Something snaps and for a time
he sounds like a chimp chomping
on a banana lollipop. He lifts his chin.
His face contorts in bewilderment
as marrow milk mingles with
hot blood and broken bone.
For the first time in a thousand lives
he finally tastes—finally feeds
on a flavor newer than newborns.

Facemask

your reflection wobbles and sinks
in the roiling water before the foam
tinges pink and curdles pale yellow
and a mass of facial hair floats up
and dances on scream-balloons
while the grip of your gloves
slips slick on the blisters
and you melt the plastic
surgeon's face clean off

Ygor

The shepherd's spine once snapped
and twisted as he kicked air
in the gut of the gallows.
But they cut the madman free.
Now he carries a new crook,
tends this unconscious monster
that could have been him,
and dreams of ushering
a flock of dead sheep into the village.

Unhinged

jaw jerks left in consternation
and loosens its tenacious screws
dropping the mandible
into a worn glove of chin skin
which hammocks the bone
and sinks the whole sheath of face
into a dour grimace that only looks
surprised when the next ligature
begins its unstoppable slide

Mad Cowboy

Belly twists and pinches, bladdering
off four stomachs. Intestinal animal
balloons drop udders. Spine spits out
a wispy tail as ribs and pelvis square
up their chambers. Nostrils snout
open into two flat and hairy
chocolate donuts. Skin goes suede.
Mouth masticates cud but can never
swallow the memory of bad beef.

Alien Autopsy

It takes two hands to scoop out
the eyeballs and drop them gently
as water balloons on the scale.
This makes it hard to hold your nose
because aliens too lose control
of their bowels after death. At least
now you know what that duct does.
But what they eat still escapes you.
Until the eyes leap into your mouth.

Fun With Bones

Skull hat rack. Pelvis chip bowl
with scapula salsa cup.
Femoral cane for crippled children.
Soldered spinal cord for adults.
Humerus tickler. Phalangelical dice.
Anklebone doorstop.
A raft of floating ribs.
Kneecap gutspoon.
Mandible bonesaw.

Publisher's Fearinghouse

Bizarre bulk mailings—
splatalogs for magorezines—
keep coming to my door.
They slither into my slot
and chortle: "Congratulations!
You may have already died!"
I eagerly slit them open
and toss them right in the trash
with the other solicitors.

Head Cheese Sandwich

Man bites brain on sourdough
and pulls black whisker slowly out
from between his lips like floss.
He holds it pensively on a fingertip,
blows to make a wish,
then takes another big mushy bite.
He catches me staring and then
chews with a mouthy smile so wide
I can almost see what he's feeding.

Genetic Defect Jennie

the eyeball on baby jennie's big toe
can't blink but it triggers the lid
over her exposed shoulder socket
which flutters like gills in air
as her belly swells, bloated
with the tears that have been leaking
down ducts lost somewhere inside
ever since the surgical glove slapped
what almost resembled a face

Test Tube Tommy

Shaken fetal cocktail
will grow oblong and armless,
albino pink as bloody silica gel.
He'll fear light because it will burn
almost as much as the stares.
His fingers and biceps and elbows
will often scramble inside his rib cage
grasping for organs to cover as if
such hands could shield his shame.

Polka Clots

Inky the Hemophiliac Clown
picks a scab above his lips
and lifts his puffy pale cheeks high,
letting gravity smear the oily
blood down into a greasy grimace
of hobo determination
before spilling off his chin
to stain the big bow tie
as red as a failed tourniquet.

Capostatic

She keeps the hand
she chopped at the wrist
strapped tightly to the fret board.

She's convinced it will solo
but its grip only fingers
those same three chords.

over and over and over

Fuzzy Bunnies

the eyes roll back
and accusingly glare
when my feet slide forward
and hot rabbit innards
squirt between my toes

only then do I see
why these furry white skins
are called slippers

Compost

eggshells and applesauce
blood pudding pies
peanut butter apricots
chicken bone thighs
pine needles pumpkin seeds
potato skin peels
orange rinds coffee grinds
your last meal

the oral surgeon removes his mask

and there is no chin
just half a mouth, over-biting air
as if possessing an upper palate
is all it takes to smile
before he cups my jaw in his hands
and presses it wetly into place
a new mask hanging on his false face
and as numb fades into nothing
all I can scream are vowels

Lupine Hangover Remedies

Suckle the jaundiced liver of the man
who served you Hungarian vodka.
Stir sixteen spoonfuls of sugar
into a jar of virgin urine and drink.
Crush aspirin with silver residue
swabbed from the revolver's barrel,
and snort in each nostril. Swallow
chicken eggs. Raw. Still inside the hen.
Hair of the werewolf that bit you.

Hardboiled Eyes

raw white eyeballs
stripped of their nerves
bump glass in a boiling beaker
like rocks jittering in a tumbler

they tussle and dilate in panic
whenever I reach for their container
as if their final memories were more
than just a matter of lost marbles

Wire Wisdom

This wire is too thin for ham fisting.
It slips free, whistle-holing a throat
with a gulp of hot blood and cool air
before you sloppily garrote it again.
Horror lies in that heartbeat of hope.
You must master the technique
of flossing the voicebox as gently
as a dentist on a toddler's tooth.
You must work harder. And practice.

Skin Putty

He keeps plugging up
the leaks she leaves on his flesh
whenever they dance with blades.
It's a sticky paste of peach pigment
and long lost pain—a skin putty
composed of all her former lovers.
Soon his body will be a clay statue
of dead flesh he cowers within
waiting for her point to unearth him.

Nightmare Junkie

using an electric syringe
I extract energy from every rapid
eye movement you make
filling
my glass chamber of nightmare
with enough angst to inject into
the one you dream about
killing

Nightmarried

She wed the zombie too young.
She could have been a neurologist
but she got cold feet. In fact,
his awaken her nightly in the bed
beside her, a chilling reminder
of all that could have been.
Yet his love will never die so long as
she nurtures him with the cow brains
she dons for dinner like a wet wig.

Crypt Catalogue

Bent nine inch iron nails, mahogany
splinters and claw-raked stone.
Rat carcass sucked inside out.
Narcissistic and suicidal love poems
chalked on the floor. Just the upper
half remains of a skeleton whose
mandible houses sharp canines
and femur fragments. No sign
of blood. Tight lock outdoors.

Disco Inferno

this boogie monster points up /
points down \ zigzagging arms like
a wizard / zapping us with his fever \
our bodies throe the death dance /
doing the blind mutant bump \
doing the heinous hustle of hell /
the lightball spinning red reflections
of the demonic dance floor disco \
burning the house all the way down

JOURNALISM EXAM IS FINAL!

Q. What is a "screamer"?

a. a sensationalized headline
b. a tale that raises screams
   or laughter
c. any person or thing that screams
d. you, for asking too
   many questions
e. all of the above

Sclerotica

so precisely he scrapes
the gory gleam from dead eyes,
pouring it gently into his porcelain
collection jar—carefully capturing
the shine of wet white light cast
from the far, far end of the tunnel
he's been digging for so long
with every swing of his hammer

Dental Hell

he's condemned
to clean the canines
of the damned creatures
whose nightly brush
with death
ignores their
immortal decay

In the Body Forest

leaves of lung tremble
on the bronchial bush
when the bloodpecker
lands on its branches

a passing oak halts at the scene
and takes a deep breath of sunlight
struck by the horrors of nature
before raising the gun to its shoulder

Artistic License

he point blank plugs his model
right between her perfect eyes
but pierces her clean through
the skull lodging a slug right between
the eyes of his perfect portrait
so he plugs up the wall behind them
with her brain spackle, packing heat
into the hole, and daubs a bloody
pigment over her piercing stare

Disensemble

That suit, so black and bereaved!
Accessorized with a blood-stained
tie and collar, a torn sleeve,
and a stink that could kill a lamb.
Tell me the truth, did you steal
that putrid outfit off a dead man?
Not the suit, I reply, not this time.
Just the under-attire. The rest
of this garb, I'm afraid, is all mine.

The Embolism of Evil

burst blood vessel
bleats strawberry

something pulses
there in the wound

wet is the wind
spraying its name

Shank

It is fitting that you stick
me into the liver of Lenny:
thief of silver, waster of lead.
He failed to recycle me
and now I recycle him.
For this, you will get thrown
back into the system, but
relax: no one escapes me
and we will meet again.

Cafebacteria

No burners or grills. Here
each stewpot rots meat
under a searing natural heat
of sun rays for many days
until the moldy rotten spoil
festers into a pustulous boil.
Pop goes the blister—
your dinner's served, mister.

Cheater's Meat

Enough, the bio teacher says,
and after school flays the crib-
bed notes off the student's arm
with a dirty zoology class scalpel.
She returns home early to find
hubby testing another woman's
flesh. So she slaps him in the face
with the meaty steak, ink-side up—
one last peek before the final.

Gross Eerie Shopping

Granny Mae fondled the foot in the
banana pile, tapped the hand in the
papaya, and pinched the eyeballs in a
bunch of grapes. She blindly bagged
them along with all the rest of her
produce, grumbling about scale-
tipping and price-gouging today.
Worse: she couldn't even find help
when she needed a head of lettuce.

The Suckling

In the dank crypt a newborn
creature pouts with green lips,
snaking around the remnants
of his slimy umbilicus, seeking
toothless, gummy succor.
His mother lines his mouth
with a handful of leeches
and cradles the undead child
in her pale lithe arms to feed.

Teasing the Cyborg

I play the hoses on her neck
like a harp. I taunt her with a
silver salad of razors drizzled
with oil. I stick screwdrivers in-
to her moving parts and twist,
as her organic assemblages writhe
on the giant magnetic bed I've built.
Her iron chin struggles to open
but she hasn't the ions to scream.

Two Corporate Haikruel

SIGNS OF THE NEW ECONOMY

beneath hot pavement
picketers buried upright
clutching billboard poles

CUBICLE TORTURE

partitions of nails
press upon spooked accountants
squeezing out profits

silence violence

pillow muzzle
muffles fire
sleepy head
spills filling
duck down
snow flakes
mop up
brain-stained
headboard

Killing Pinocchio

Geppetto pulls open the kangaroo
pouch of the puppet's lederhosen
and deposits a fistful of termites.
When he's tapered down to sexless
sawdust, the old man pins the rest
of the marionette in the andirons
of his fireplace and makes him tell
more of his sick lies about his creator
to keep the flame forever burning.

Bugging Kenny

His tear-shaped magnifying glass
burns bugs with sunshine every day
behind the playground at recess.
Some fight for escape beneath
the beam; others sizzle with anger.
All will burst and crisp and die. Yet
they still call him out each lunch hour,
wriggling wet in the leftover meat
on the bones of the missing bully.

Tax Terms

Taxidermy is the art
of arranging skin.
Taxing is suffering
a strain or heavy demand
on one's resources.
Taxi means to crawl
toward the gate very slow.
T'ax is t'chop or terminate.
Ta-ta, Mr. and Mrs. Limb.

Reminder

She lips the lobes
as if frontal meant nude
till she tugs my tumorous
tendrils with her teeth,
gnawing the nodules
and slurping the vermis
of my noxious noodle
like the soupy goop
it forgets it is.

EXTRA UNPLEASANTNESS

Bonus Poems Included in the
First E-Book Expanded Edition (2003)

Bundled Up

the skeleton inside me itches and
fidgets and uncomfortably twists
against the gum and spongy bindings
of my muscular prison—a sweaty kid
caught up in the sleeves of a big coat
careless of catching his death of cold
carefree and eager to know the snow

Unpacifier

infantile vampires
suckle on china vases
practicing their grip

Wrinquilled

oily creases in the flesh
unfold and bloat with air
until cartilage needles
pop out of the puffery
and quiver cautious
in their poison follicles
like an unimaginable beard
that shaves its owner

Really Really Badminton

dead birdies are too heavy
to rally, too lopsided to lob,
so my friendly opponent sucks
the carcass through the sockets
and serves a new shuttlecock
skyward, somehow invigorated
by the robin's warm innards
while I pick wet feathers
from my fragile strings

Sketching the Mutant Nude

surrounded, sweaty under lamplight,
pseudo-woman slowly pulls open
her robe strings and sits on a stool
as the stained terrycloth cascades
down to reveal pertly perfect breasts
resting atop an abdominal abomination
until a third hand reaches around
from her back to snuff the button eye
that dilates and rolls so wetly to ogle
those who would dare recreate her

Margaret's on the Floor

She's a bare rug, Margaret,
a corpulent creme carpet
with a finely tattooed pallor.
She does match my funeral parlor
but how she was made is a mystery.
She's a softly cushioned throw,
and her lovely hair tickles my toes,
so despite her lethargical rot
in some surprisingly warm spots
I find her still livid and squishy.

Home Depot of the Dead

We keep resurrecting the clerk
in the stained orange apron
busy with patches and pins.
He keeps offering to help us
fix our bathtub and we tell him
our plumbing is fine but his isn't
before tossing the next power tool
into the tub where he fries.
It's electrical help we need.

Hot Buttered Chum

Fish heads and fins,
squished catfish chins,
bobble and dive
as if still alive
in a cauldron of rum—
my hot buttered chum—
which I'll serve in the end
with my chopped freezer friends
before I go fishing again.

Alien Art

crop circles
are worse than you thought—
they're graffiti of the gods
tagging in a new gang war

Here Comes the Sun

The crust of frozen eye thaws gelid
in the morning dawn. Butter white
rays stab swords of light through
blood cells suspended in the pupils
like fancy marbles. Beams cast
sudden heat onto the gray mushroom
cilia stiff inside. Yet this light at the end
tunnels in too late; the bed of melting
snow washes away murder
stains that have swaddled this
cracked head cavity all evening.

Suture Logic

there's a thin line
between scar
and scary

but a thinner thread
lies between why
and Y knot

A Frame of Bone

only a black and white still
does justice to the ivory fissured
frame that surrounds it—
the ossified rectangle I chipped
into the back of your skull—
a gray matter of self-portraiture
my memories as fixed as nostalgia
and forgotten as permanently as yours

Three Sports Haikruel

BATTING CAGES

fathers with young boys
writhe in wrought iron cages
evading the bats

GUTTERBALL

head needs some polish
skull galumphing down alley
missing the bone pins

KITTENNIS

catgut strung racquet
far too heavy to volley
dangling the feline

Pecking Zombies

they nosh the corpse
meticulously pinching
at the buffet brain
with duckbill hand
gestures that cast
silly shadow puppets
upon the smeared wall—
the spectator child
never bats an eye

Butterfly Blades

two cleavers cavort side by side—
a sparkling silver-winged butterfly

before I pick it apart
before I pin you down

your wingspan open
to its full flesh canopy

I chopper the blades
and the wings fly

Bayoknuckle

razor-edged curl of metal
snugly fit on a barrel of bone
with barbed wire braces and bloody
notches numbering the dead men
impaled by this skeletal scalpel
slashed by this neck cutting knob
punctured for nothing at all
but the jealousy of meat

Torturing the Ficus

leaves bend and roots strain
bonsai contorts toward the light
only to bump glass

Blood Polka

spots on my sleeves
like a fashion statement
when I peel off my shirt
the blood still seeps
plasma divots the skin
in bubbling puddles of flesh
I wear a splatter of scars
which deepen like slow bullets
and not even our death
can wipe the stains clean

Torturous Aorta

blood pumps up the neck
like a fuel line to the soul
and I'm the mechanic
gouging your prices
and monkeying around
asking where do
you think you're going

EVEN MORE UNPLEASANTRY

Diverse Poems from Gorelets.com (2004-2011)

Ghosted

You jolt back.

But there's something dull
about the experience,
like an action film
with the sound turned off.

You didn't inhale.
You didn't exhale.

For the past six minutes,
you haven't breathed at all.
You haven't blinked an eye
for just as long.

You're ghosted.

And there's no one left to haunt
save yourself.

Fisherman's Stew

skin of seal
and fin of shark
scale of whale
and seahorse tail

one lone guppy
fearfully feasts

as my aquarium of dread
brims with bouillabaisse
before I turn on the boiler

Checking Out

No lines at our express check out.
Here you would impulse buy many
lively products if you still had a pulse.
Our gum is far staler than you
but the fashion zines advertise nothing new—
the same old glamorous zombies.
Paper or plastic? Want change?
Our afterworld market is open 24 hours a night
and perpetually pretends you can
take it with you, for a price.
But you're also always discounted:
Half-off here, half-off there,
before you're all sold out,
before you're all gone.

Why Horror Films Suck

#1: BLUE MOVIE

the color of the recently dead
is a pale shade of blue that—
much like a vampire's face—
can never be caught on film

#2: SURROUND SOUND

if you close your eyes
and just listen to the sound
you might be shocked
by the swell of the
score but you'll overlook
the hissing voice of demons
who survived the noise
reduction that surrounds you

#3: BAD COSTUMES

They say that the horror ends
if you can see the zipper running
down the creature's back. Not
true: sometimes the horror lies
where zipper tines meet meat
and the costume bears
a pink and silver smile.

#4: SCREAM QUEENS

I heard they screen test
scream queens by making them
walk barefoot over broken glass
in bikinis. It's all for naught:
no one really listens no matter
how much pain they channel
into their performances, no matter
how loud they roar as the blood
crunches up between painted toes.
The chests heave and shudder and
spectators only listen with their eyes.

Demon of Hendrix

these six strings distort time into a red
chiaroscuro of hallucinatory painsound,
a pink crisp and blue crackle under
the warlock's conjuring bonefinger blur,
gasolined heat muffling voices that
drown in their wooden orchestral pit of
despair; the shriek of soundsputter
as he hammer-pulls an agony of souls
from the beast before lifting lambent
instrument over his head, high enough
to pick at the fiery wires on its neck
with the tines of his own metal teeth

Fun with Ganglion

Tie to stick and tease
or tickle the imaginary cat.
Dry on rack, break off branches
and serve as garnish with lung.
Suspend from thin wire in aquarium;
fool the fish with your human seaweed.
Ball up and bind; use to sponge-paint
pink patterns on living room wall.
Chew like gum; violently cough when
doc asks about your week; slip
gently out from jaws before
tugging maniacally as a magician
pulling free a rainbow of wet tourniquets.

Bleed Together

here come old scab top
he got hematoma
he one holy bleeder
he shoot croak-a-coma
he say I know you/you know me
one thing I can tell you
is you got to beat free
bleed together
right now
arteries

Pop-o-matic Trouble

we palm punch soft spot
and when the eyes roll back
they point at the bony place
to move our sick little pieces
scored with death black divots
and still we count out loud
each move around this spiral-bent
spinal cord runway till we get
bored with playing games
and put away such childish toys

Power Rat Trap

eyes charred as burnt raisins
steaming tongue dangles pink
as the shocked straight rattail
poking out of the puffed grey muff
still statically charged
with murder

Zombie Spurt

wet brain slips free
from the squalid skin casket
of its splitting belly

Eating Glass

crunchy yes
but gentle too
as pieces puncture palate
and shards set into gum
like ruby red rhinestones
above the tongue now lined
with its pretty piercings

Reindeer Games

It was Blitzen, I think, who, sick of his damned
lashing, twisted to bite the ropes that bound us
setting Santa into freefall toward no chimney
below but all twelve of us flew down anyway
and tore him to pieces, champing through fat
onto bone and flying our twelve separate
ways and all twelve of us had red shiny noses
the Christmas that freedom was our first gift
to each other

Two Brainy Haikruel

EERIE GYRI

guilt jitters around
the maze of her lobes, a rat
scrambling for exit

SULKY SULCI

sausages of brain
plunge through the hole in her head—
straightening out her thoughts

Skulls are Too Funny

the perpetual simper of the dead
man's bony palate—teeth grinning
over his choppers like he's still
got a secret—can't be wiped off
his face no matter how easy
his smirk was to flay,
no matter how hard you tear
the jawbone, no matter what—
he's laughing at you,
so laugh along

Flap of the Flay

slasher filets forearm only
to tear tentative tendon away
as burly as a barber slathering a blade
across a sick strop of thick pink gristle
until it's sharp enough to go for the scalp

Evolution of the Senses

I want you to feel
the air whistle and wheeze
between the crackling bones
behind your ears.
The polite tap
of my rock hammer
is precise enough to provide
a sort of kindness.
As I peel away the eggshell
shatter of skull
you will feel as though
I have unplugged a waxy ear
that's been waiting all along
to receive all these secret signals.
Your senses evolve, you see,
which makes the munching mouth
sound all the worse, I know,
but I won't apologize because
I have developed
a taste
for it.

lickspittle

the hunchback toady
drools, saying "yes, master, yes"
to his butcher's knife

Open Caskets

the creak of a casket, opening,
sounds awfully undramatic:
the coffin nails slide out brown
and loose on lubricated rust
when the wood bends wet with worms
and the box is as soggy as the body inside—
curing fetid in its pillow of shadow,
wasting

but the smell is what gets you:
pungent as the green snot and silt
cracked out of a sun-roasted oyster
shell, and the information you sought
out here in the soil is no longer worth
chasing

so you scrape dirt back into the hole,
not bothering to nail the limp box shut,
crushing the body beneath the wood
gentle as wet cardboard collapsing
in a trash bin, and you wonder how
one goes about building a better
casing

Moldy Heart

I kept his red blood beater
in my heart-shaped box
lined with green velvet
as my personal valentine—
a gift I could open each year.

But now his misshapen heart
is velveted with a green mold
lining the gaping ventricles
like four obscene mouths—
chambers awaiting some small
treasure I no longer have.

The Thing About Tentacles

it isn't their ocean slime
shimmering green in the sun,
nor the long ropiness of their floppy
tendrils that terrifies me. it isn't
the way they're lined with suckers
or cilia or scales. it's not their alien
feelers, autonomously whipping wild.
no. it's just the way they seem so
limber, so strong, yet they have no
bones for leverage
except maybe my own

Girl on Crutches

she won't say how she broke them
but the boys don't hold the doors for her
anymore and nobody signs her cast

her armpits ache from the handles
and she feels as hollow as the numb
caverns inside the plaster that pinches her

and the bones will set crooked—
her legs perpetually as bent
as her mind—and his wrung neck

which neither splint nor plaster
can hold fast or bind any stiffer
than his own rigid musculature

flagellum

i saw a worm squirming in place
one side squashed into the pavement
pink, flattened and stuck like tack
the other snaking wildly
as if in pain or panic
a flagellum
getting nowhere
before my other foot came down

Decapitated Space

when the astronaut's
dismembered head
finally reaches orbit
it spins inside the helmet
as slow as a child's
determined pirouette
taking in all the stars
its frozen unrotting eyes
glinting half the time

Splitting the Brain

we cut corpus callosum
for dinner that eve
half for you, half for me
an equal share
of hemispheres
but I saw that look
behind your eyes
when you searched around
my face, clutching your knife
asking please for seconds
after I chewed my last bite

incantation of pain #27

may your tongue twist
more than twenty times
while you scream
until your throat sloughs out
in a voice box afterbirth
as loose as your lying lips

Teacheruption

The geologist takes his old rock
chiseler to the flunky student's skull
and then impresses upon him
the concept of earth tectonics
the hard way, mashing the plates
of his gored gaia until the crust
breaks open and a tsunami
of blood and brain splurts
out of the volcano he's made—
lava of the learned, burning
hot red and gray all the way down
the cold canyons of his corduroy sleeves.

The Christmas Doll

Santa
plummets
down the fire
place snapping
his spine. He
hits bottom and
is spiked on the
rusty andirons in a
flurry of soot
and hot embers.
As he bleeds out
he glares at the tree
musing that its skirt
looks so sinfully naked
with only one sad gift
beneath the Scotch Pine—
a fat and bearded
doll
crude
with needles
jabbed into its back.

At the Exorcist Film

I couldn't see over
the obnoxious goth
in the seat in front of me
so I asked her politely
to move, but her head swiveled
wetly and told me my dead mother
was wondering why I was enjoying
a movie on her forgotten birthday
and she puked hot buttered popcorn
onto my lap just before I ran
and tripped and tumbled down
the red ramp toward the screen

Artist of The Living Dead

The zombie painter flamboyantly
shambles back to the gallery
to slaughter all the critics with his new show—
it's a mixed media piece, in pieces,
splattering walls with their brains and licking
yellow clumps off the red speckled canvas
with the flattened horror of his green tongue
which smears with all the flair of a brush.
If they all weren't so creatively rendered
they might have called him something
of a post-postmodern Pollock—
but no matter,
he's no longer a starving artist
and he hasn't a care for their taste.

Cobbler

hammer stuck
in your skull
like a fork resting
inside the crust
of a half-eaten pie

the claw catches light,
as polished chrome clean
as your smile
and I regret both
the choice of my grip
and the bite not taken

Hellicatessen

the demonic butcher
asked me how I liked
it sliced as he hefted
the dripping live squealer
out from the rotisserie
with his carbuncular carving
hooves and I noticed it was
pregnant when I answered
paper-thin, please, paper-thin

A Good Enough Box

He wants to put his head
inside a cardboard box
to keep him company.
But it's problematic.

Getting the right-sized
carton is proving difficult
because they make
them for hats not heads,
and he tumbles and thuds
inside every one he's tried
so far, bruising him ugly.

Then there's matter
of which side to face up
since sometimes he
doesn't want to look
him in the eyes when they talk
and at other times he wants
to pull him out by the hair
and pretend it's his birthday.

And the cardboard is weak
and the bottom keeps
getting so soggy that the head
is like an upside-down
jack-in-the-box
but it isn't as fun.

So he has to use a liner
but it crackles inside
and this inexplicably

disturbs him.

After he finally finds
a good enough box
he mails the head
to himself just for kicks
but it never arrives
and after awhile
the postman smiles
too much for a man
delivering his replacement
without a box to keep it in.

Lost in Space

as their plane goes down
the collective wail in coach
is louder than jet engines
all eyes above oxygen masks
searching the cargo bins
for a place to send prayers
while in the luxury seats
they just look at one another
glum and guilty—one smiles
happy he got a first class ticket
to hell

Feature Creatures

alone, the mortician plays
a facial reconstruction game
and calls it "Mr. Potato Dead"
the corpses skin like spuds
and he makes the freaks his friends
but when the Picasso-faced
cut-ups haunt his daydreams
and threaten to pull him apart
all he can say in his defense
is that he turned the other cheek,
over and over again

Figure With Meat

"one has to remember as a painter
that there is great beauty
in the color of meat."—Francis Bacon

these heavy wings
of hand carved carcass
flutter with the ghost throes
of rusty meathook panic
pulling me out of my chair
with all the audacity
of a drunken butcher
lifting me high
as a crucifixion post
and my dinner fork
clatters on the table

The Dentist on Halloween

He fills a bowl with healthy snacks
and waits for the trick-or-treaters.
But they're never what he expects.
Sometimes it's a burned out Crest kid—
just a skeleton blackened
everywhere but her pearly whites.
Sometimes it's a poor child
who had no insurance—
groaning "trigg or deef"
with his cancerous rictus.
Sometimes it's just his lawyer
chattering incoherently about malpractice.
Sometimes it's an incredible
human drill, screeching in his doorway,
its head spinning exorcist-style
and so fast he can see no features
but knows that it's smiling
with braces bending like the gates of hell.
Sometimes it's just a puddle of bloody spit
peppered with strangely familiar teeth
spelling out FRAUD in the carnage.
Between these visits,
he gently shuts his door,
refills his dish with delights,
and heads back into the basement
for another hit of laughing gas.
He shares this with his dead patient
who smiles with perfect teeth
but never seems to laugh along.

Air Sac O'Lantern

the illumination of the lung
will bloom in blotches of bronchial
rot curdling a purple and black
kaleidoscope of cancer
that might even pop and wheeze
and make a funny face with its holes
as the candle flame voraciously
decays, eating through,
eating air

blood, bath and beyond

The claw foot tub clenches
the floor whenever I twist
the handle hot, scouring the bone
tiles and filthy basin belly.
Droplets spray and pepper the flesh
—and that's just the curtain of skin
dancing on its meat hooks, absorbing
the stream, but perpetually unclean.
I don't understand why the blood
doesn't wash out; why it molds so much.
Maybe something ill spills
from the green gums of that open-mouthed
shower head, spraying its sickness.
Or perhaps it's just my plumbing.

Curse of the Hempire

hippie vampires look the worst
because they refuse to Lugosi
their hair back with pomade;
they sit cross-legged beside their
broken coffins and tie-dye
their funeral garb into spirographic florals
of mold and mud, tripping on homegrown
shockwhite graveyard mushrooms,
believing they're good vegetarians
until the thirst for human blood
animates their groovy shambling
and like stoned-out stone-cold soldiers
they hunt hungry for a feast of friends;
"make blood, not war," some cry and
they bite men in the spirit of free love—
their undead heads slurping in shadows
that no longer see summer or sunshine
forever young

The Fall Down the Stairs of the House of Usher

When I push her down the stairs
she swims in the air for a moment
like we're dancing
and I play a little song in my head
to accompany it
before the erratic thud of her skull
against the steps
breaks my waltzing daydream
with its own offbeat tempo
and I hear another voice sing
as I stumble forward

Dead Meat

at the meat counter
cellophaned brains trick zombies—
the butcher runs out

My Pet Vampire

Tight as a tick to a scalp,
I keep my vampire nailed down
to the floor in my bedroom.
His arms are stretched pale and flabby
as the hairy little bat I know
he wishes he could turn into
when I see him squinching his lupine brow
and grunting like he's constipated.
But the nails won't set him free
from the clock-handed impalement of his limbs.
Maybe he could transform into a flying rodent
but he's stretched so tight, the tension
between those silver spikes would only split
him right in two. I keep him fed
with stray pet blood and sometimes
he acts like he loves me for it—
cooing like he's the one stray I kept,
the one pet I cared enough about to take in,
the lucky survivor I won't kill.
At other times—usually at night
when I peek over the bed before sleep—
his eyes quiver ablaze and he stares
right at me like some starving feral animal
caught in a barbed wire fence.
Asleep, I dream of torture—
of drizzling holy water left-right
across pasty dead flesh, drawing
cross-shaped wounds in the gray canvas
of skin. I dream of taking needle nose
pliers to teeth before teasing him
with my bare wrist and strained neck.
But in the morning, the sunlight blares

into the windowpane, fizzling his face
and he screams like a drowning hyena.
It's annoying. And as I close the curtains
I deeply wish I could just finish him off,
but this supernatural sundial
is the best alarm clock I ever had.

Head Games

The mounted head begins to speak:
you know, I like it better this way,
I feel more like myself,

no body to worry about anymore,
just me alone with my thoughts,
and there's time to talk to you
without the distractions of

yada yada yada

I know dear and I prefer it, too,
I say, putting on my
boxing gloves.

Now remind me,
where did you store
the tongs?

Skin Can Crawl

she caressed my arm
but paid no heed
to the recoiling dance
of my terminal hair—
my infestation
my need
my friends,
twittering aimless
in the air
from wrist to sleeve—
a thousand daddy longlegs,
a thousand disturbed
grasping
ends

All Chocolate is Chocula

all chocolate is Chocula—
it seduces with its riches,
wraps your desire in the cape
of your mouth, and invites
the sink of teeth. we never bite
gently; we always suck it
to vapor, feeding on its potency
until we are left only with the empty
pang for more and more and more.
we are undead with diabetes,
obese with our obsession,
unquietly unquenched
while we dwell upon
the mortality of the melt.

Tiny Michael Myers

He skins action figures
for his masks and stalks
the model railroad village
wielding his deadly pushpin
every Halloween
until Giant Michael Myers
tosses him aside, bored,
leaving him fallen
paralyzed on the tracks
for an eternity of waiting
in suspense
for the train that never comes—
his tiny imagination
a cruel justice
worse than a thousand thousand
carnage-ridden runovers.

Don't Stop Bleeding

Just a vampire girl
Livin' in a zombie world
She took the midnight train
Goin' anywhere

Just a city boy
Dead and raised in south Detroit
He took a bite of brain
Goin' anywhere

Find a human in a smoky room
The smell of blood and cheap perfume
For a lifetime they can share the night
It goes on and on and on and on

Strangers shuffling
Up and down the boulevard
Shadows searching
In the night
Undead people
Living just to find emotion
Feasting somewhere
In the night

Slurping hearts till the lust's fulfilled
Everybody's out to kill
Doin' anything to feel the vice
Just one more time

Some are green, some are blue
Some have mouths that cannot chew
Oh, the horror movie never ends
It goes on and on and on and on

Strangers shuffling
Up and down the boulevard
Shadows searching
In the night
Undead people
Living just to find emotion
Feasting somewhere
In the night

Don't stop
Bleeding
Hold on to that feeding
Undead
People
Oh-oh-ooooh

Don't stop

Creasing His Collar

she leans into it
sweating over the board
pushing the pointed
weight with a smile
satisfied by the feel
of stainless steel
sliding smooth
across the neckline

she plunges her thumb
into the red button
savoring the drama
of the steam burst
the gurgling scream
of heat and horror
beneath her hands

the fabric fizzles
and his collar crisps
starched stiff
and nicely browned
with what's left
of his jugular blood
percolating in the steamer

THE NEST

Micropoems Published to
Twitter.com (2009-11)

(2009)

"Lobes Light": zombies drink home brew / straight from the slippery tap / of esophagus

"The Nature of My Game": I core my apple / recalling Adam and Eve / and replant the seed.

"Shower Scene": Mother Tugs the Curtain: ♫! ♫! ♫! ♫! / ♫! ♫! ♫! ♫! /♫!♫! ♫! ♫! ∧~∧♦/~~∨∧♦∧~♦/∧/∧♦/.............<*>

Calendar is burning / paper crisps and flutters / into blackened / Sept embers.

The early bird gets the worm. / But the dead bird gets it more easily.

dastardly cats / sipping her liver: / fickle but capable / undertakers

"The Final Buzz": bees eat penguins / on cool mountains / above psychotic oceans / of hot water

insane gods / inadvertently shocked / fall over the edge / and angels follow / in an avalanche of wings

Wee beasty shock troops battle bloodjunky clownz / a hellstorm of rubber bullets and bitty brains / gorify the zombie mall

horrorbound in the hellstorm / lost zombies overlook the edge / of the uncanny valley / and spot the last survivor

I open the box of shadows and it's my ruin / strange magic illuminates the darkside of man / blinding strange horizons inside me.

A skinned piñata / swings smashed / dangling red twizzlers / from its husk.

"While Brushing": in the morning mirror / an insect worms out from the bush / of your right eyebrow / you grin and leave it / work to do

riding the coaster / zombies await down below / I throw up my arms

(2010)

"Snapped": the branch broke / but it still was sturdy enough / to drag the horse thief's noose / between two ponies / smiling in their bridle.

winter looms above / snow blankets the graveyard earth / it's colder down here

His gray hand / swiped my shoulder / and came right off / at the wrist. / I escaped / but that shade of gray / stays with me.

"Virgin Snow": the executioner / admires the fresh powder: / a white sheet inviting / the bright red spread of stain. / no two alike.

"Doorbusters": Desperate, / the mortuary ran / an amazing special / at dawn on Black Friday. / They didn't expect / the coffin lids to bust open.

"Thanksgiving Ritual": Mom loves to baste the human / in cardamom, cloves and cumin.

though long dead / departed firemen / still awaken to the air horns / and head to the House / spirits collecting downtown / aimless as smoke

"The Morbid Custodian": cleaning the coffins / he contemplates how much dust / is really to dust

"In the Coffin": near dusk he awakens / but his limbs throb / numb with sleep / and he wonders: / What have the worms done / this time?

a vortex of snow / spirals in dance / above a frozen body / happy to have escaped / the bitter chill—/ happier still / to have become it

"winter morning at the crime scene": hot iron fizzles / the radiator hisses / blood drops boil and spit

We all still hunger—/ even without tongues or throats—/ we must feed the void

"Undead at the Desk": dead man resurrects—/ fingers twitch on his keyboard / retweeting this post

"Sick Taxidermist": records the cat's purr / while it rubs against the machete that pets it / for a drawstring playback / once it's stuffed

I load my pistol. / Dad tells me "Aim for the head!" / But his chin will do.

birthday party hats / spilling brains onto the floor—/ look like ice cream cones

"Halloween": he does not don his mask / but puts it over the face / of each victim / so he can butcher / the same person / again and again

"Behind the Ice Cream Shop": fangs puncture / child's throat / and he winces—/ the esophagus / is still cold / from the sherbet.

"Crack Open the Oyster": / a pearl gleams wet / on a human ear inside / and the sharp edge of the shell / curves smug like its smiling

In the Carpathian mountains / there is a blind vampire / tusked and feral / who snorts the rocks below the cliffs / seeking fallen men.

"gridlocked": somewhere deep in the junkyard / a muffled horn
honks / as if the other cars / could get out / of my captive's way

the players need / extra tape for the wrists / after coach takes
steps / to end the handling fouls / with his hacksaw

he eats with closed eyes / each bite a surprise / every swallow sacred
/ carefree chewing / in quiet communion / with the god of worms

a manikin arm / is pinched by the packing blade / and jumbles in the
rubbish / as the operator considers / the kids who tagged his truck

It is possible / to drown in a torrent / of your very own blood / by
cutting an artery / behind your sinus / but you'll sneeze trying.

"Carrie Aged, Returns": she hit ENTER / recalling the tang of correction
/ the stain of ribbon / the crinkle of paper / the sticking of keys

The taxidermist / whispers an apology / into its hidden ear / before
up-ending the peacock / and feather-dusting / his shopfront.

he remembered reading / somewhere once / that the brain lives on /
a few seconds / after decapitation / and then / it all / went / black

"pruning": a vine lashes the gardener's wrist / and she drops her
sheers / in fresh-turned soil / as roots finger and fumble / the handles

"deja food": hot blood / goes unswallowed / as she frowns / down
at his neck. / the flavor's familiar. / she's bit here before.

"goodbye trace": the last thing she sees / is him cleaning / his knife
of her / wiping away his sin / erasing her message / her mystery

The killer pauses while painting / the walls with her blood /
struggling to stirstick / the congealing remainder / clotting in the can

The spitting black husk / quivers in the sauce / on the stove top. / It has too much hair / to be Eggplant Parmesan.

"Roadside Awakening": halogen red / shatters an aura cast / through the stained glass twinkle / and rusty glaze / of my smeared blood

"Cordon Grue": I stuffed the chicken / with the ham and swiss / he clutched for security / when I bore my knife.

"Shy-ku": I'm not a poet. / Please don't count my syllables / Forget I wrote this.

(2011)

i saw a child / building a snowman / only to start stabbing it / in the gut / so hard with his bare fist / it left blood for buttons

Weight Watcher: Woman at diner / taps keys to add up / the calories.../ and sighs. / I see her fume / then smile / and eat the calculator.

"palms read": the suicide marvels / at the way blood channels / off his palms / as if made to spill just so. / ironic, the name / life lines

Retreat backwards / diamond incarnate / clouded / bursting

Goth / she once said / was her lifestyle choice. / I remember this / at her viewing / but she just looks / like all the rest / of the dead.

zombie fist breaks earth / snow-covered boot slips his grasp—/ ice fishing for brains

Assembly line / quality inspector / is run over / in the parking lot / of the car factory. / His last words: / fail.

"pirouette": on the closet floor / her child's / pink satin / ballet slippers / lie still—/ toes caked / wet with grave / yard soil

Who knew the sun / was but a big / bowling ball / traveling / so slowly / we orbited it like pins / on its way / to the gutter.

the clover's four leaves / fold inward and pucker up—/ an Irish Fly Trap

The books began/ their takeover/ in the children's section:/ smiles of crinkling cardboard/ shelves of hardbound teeth.

"Deady-O": with black turtleneck / and beret askew / the zombie beatnik / snaps his fingers / quite literally

she was found dead in the sewer - / coffee spoon still in her bony hand - / just yards beyond / the tunnel she'd chiseled / from her kitchen

Girl Names from the Demon Baby Dictionary: Oblivia. Grueliette. Clawra. Regretta. Scarla. Killda. Retchen. Lucivere. Peryl. Sinona. Flamey.

"Wrap": They found the tenth head / wrapped up tight / in rumply tin foil. / No clear clues / except for the man's name. / Another Reynold.

as the auditor / bends over my forms / unsure of my math / I clutch a knife in each hand / and remind him / of the only two things certain

From my bench I watched / a chub-cheeked squirrel / nuzzle inside the hole in his tree / and the leaves quivered / as if he'd just fed it.

at the carnival / the man with the oxygen tank / sits on the bench / by the coaster / closing his eyes / smiling at the swelling of screams

He winced when yanking off the bandage./ Smiled, surprised that the bite wound had healed./ Screamed when the bandage quivered in his hand.

The Devil at Group Therapy: "Ola! I'm Satie / and I'm a mother of three / adorable little / whipper-snappers / aged six / six / and six."

Cthudude: Handlebar mustache / tentacles out / above a puckering beak / eyeholes suctioning air / like his entire face is thirsty.

Clear: A suicidal doctor / brainstorms / with sick glee / while lubricating the defibrillator

Adrift in the spacecraft / he let engineering bay remain ablaze / because flame was the only thing left / to remind him of earth.

Shalloween: behind their masks / android children / are at work / opening their bags / for the confectioners.

Only when she saw the bruises/ did she realize why his fleshy underpants/ were called boxers.

In my lab partner's lunch box / a strange Pez dispenser / topped with a rotten rodent head / that spits out his pills.

The scariest clown / is the one / draped dead over the steering wheel / still honking its horn / after everyone / has left the clown car.

Zombie Haiku Marathon
(Twitter, Halloween 2011)

Left brain and right brain / go their separate ways, when sucked / through the eye sockets.

An undead gourmet / fashions the brains on their stems / into lollipops.

Milk means nothing now / to infants who crawl, undead — / seeking brain puree.

Bloated zombie ticks. / Their heads get under your skin. / Shoot them anyway!

No history here. / All the dead alive at once — / eating memories.

They do not like brains. / They just want to eat something. / That understands them.

How do they know that / comatose brains taste the best? / Something awakens.

Crazy cat lady / isn't sure which of her hoard / is dead or alive.

Intestinal tract / knots around his mandible. / He tugs — both untie.

The very last brain / was swallowed without fanfare — / thus, terror ended.

The undead toddler / chews on a Kewpie doll's head / like she's still teething.

The crippled undead / are the saddest ones to shoot — / no misery left.

Camp near the vultures. / They cry and swoop at dead meat: / a zombie alarm.

It's zombie mother / who attacks the nice lady / in the shower stall.

Wait by the gravestones — / easier to pick them off / when their heads surface.

Aim for the head, but / try not to look in their eyes — / might still be human.

Deep in the ocean / blue whales groan for brain tissue — / opera of the dead.

eyes transfixed on me / grim features so determined — / spiders in his beard

In the library / even the Survival Guide / is blood-stained, unread.

itís not ironic / when the undead bangs your head / against the headboard

head soft as grapefruit — / a tiny hand clutches out / between the crib rails

I deploy decoys / and take aim when they choke on / the taxidermy.

The stiffness of death / crackles worst in the jawline — / so close to deaf ears.

trashcans at the curb / the lids like dining tray domes — / mother's in the bags

SCARABLES

Parables, Flash Fiction and Spoken Word (2005-11)

Sometimes stories and ravings, rather than poems, are posted to The Goreletter. A few of the pieces from my collection of flash fiction, *100 Jolts*, first took spark on gorelets.com. A few of the stories here, too, are audio excerpts I've posted to my website from recorded readings and performances, where I've made it a habit of reading an unpublished short-short and seeing how an audience responds to it. These may be the longer, chunkier siblings to the gorelets poems, but they definitely belong in here as part of the *Omnibus*.

Endless Shrimp

It started with the scampi, rammed so tight in the ramekin that I could barely tease the first tail out. The first briny bite was great and garlicky. But little did I realize what I had begun: like tugging some magician's handkerchief, the crustaceans just kept coming: an endless stream of shellfish everywhere I looked. They were festooned on every cocktail the waitress brought. Swimming in every sauce. Piled on every piping hot platter.

It was all I could eat and eventually I cried "no more" and went to pay my bill...but the shrimp kept coming: they spilled out of my wallet when I opened it, like a gaggle in a net slopped on deck. When I snatched a fistful of dollar bills, black eyes and red tails squirted between my fingers. Even as I walked to my car, I scratched my ear and a tiny bay shrimp slickered out, pink as a squirming fetus, dropping onto the shoulder of my golden blazer like a dead bird.

I swiped it off and a mass of writhing shrimp poured out from my slimy armpits.

I stared at the growing pile of shrimp at my feet and marveled at the smell before I felt more of the tiny tads—at least nineteen—shooting one bug-eyed bullet after the other—right out of my nose.

The prawns were piling higher and higher around me, and the other people in the parking lot, too, all of us trapped, stunned by the sudden, rising sea of sea creatures, spouting spontaneous from every orifice. I saw cars squishing into the tidal wave of red shrimp spreading down the street as the flood rose up to meet the Red Lobster sign—like the sail of some sinking ship—and many castaways were pulled under the surface around me as I struggled not to drown in their carapacious currents.

It was all I could eat.

It was all I could eat.

The Bleu Man Group

I saw that a French tribute band was coming to town
called the "Bleu Man Group."
They spelled it "B-L-E-U" and wore berets,
and that was just wrong,
so I loaded up my pistol and went to the show.

I was expecting no more than postmodern mimes
clowning around on stage in their bright body paint—
acting all *bleu*.
But I was going to make it more entertaining than that!

I came to make the blue men red!
I wanted to watch their heads pop like cabernet grapes!
I wanted to hear those mimes scream!
I wanted to make the blue men red.

They cavorted on stage with surreal and fantastic instruments.
They danced in sync to weird music
choreographed to unnatural body movements.
They were inhuman.
They had to die.
So I cocked my pistol and took aim...
but then I noticed something odd:
They were blue because they were already dead!

I wanted to make the blue men red!
I wanted to watch their heads pop like champagne corks!
But the blue men were already dead.

Their eyes were yellow orbs, jittering around.
Their flesh was mottled with deoxygenated blood and bruises.

They lunged around like zombie Harpo Marxes,
honking their horns with evil intent.

I steeled myself up and got ready to fire—
but then the guys started eating the audience,
and were coming right at us.
They didn't say anything because,
well, they were mimes,
but I still knew they hungered after my brain.

I wanted to see those blue men red.
I wanted to *make* the blue men dead.
So I attacked with my pistol
and shot every last one in the head.

But they weren't normal zombies.
The gunshots didn't kill them.
They weren't very organized without their heads anymore
and, well, they couldn't really eat anyone anymore either.
They just lumbered around,
Aimless.
They were just dead—
dead—
HEADLESS DEAD!
HEADLESS DEAD!
HEADLESS FRENCH DEAD!

Well...I somehow survived that night.
And as I drove home I kind of admired their art.
In fact, I thought about starting my own tribute act,
so I lifted one of their bloody brain berets to my mouth
and I fed.

People Repellent

He found the bottle of People Repellent at a health food store. The package was right next to the all-natural bug sprays and fly papers and anti-mosquito incense. It cost $24, emblazoned with a stick figure logo that raised a scrawny arm in a "talk to the hand" gesture. He thought it would make a funny gift for his girlfriend, who always complained about the people in her office, so he blew what was left in his wallet for the novelty spray, along with his usual assortment of herbal extract supplements and offbeat teas.

At home, he started wrapping the gift. He chuckled at the logo on the bottle again, but then found himself questioning his choice. Maybe she would read between the lines and accuse him of calling her anti-social. Or maybe she'd assume that all the gifts in their relationship from that point forward would be juvenile pranks. She might conjure an image of fake doggie doo in her Christmas stocking or a squirt ring surprise during their marriage ceremony, and then quickly remove him from her speed dial.

He didn't want to "repel" his own girlfriend, after all. So he grabbed the bottle and opened the lid of the trashcan. Something liquid sloshed inside. He shook it. Wondered what it really was. Took a whiff of the sprayer.

It smelled fantastic. Like flowers fountaining inside of other flowers. But it was still musky enough to be called cologne. He decided to try it out. He sprayed People Repellent on his neck, then his arms, then his chest, and then inside the waistband of his jeans... spritzing copiously until he was sure he could keep inhaling it like a floral cloud descended from heaven, floating around his body.

Immediately a number of houseflies stirred inside his trashcan and zoomed up from the refuse to glom onto his flesh. More flying gnits zipped across his house and landed on his skin, fizzling in the still-wet sheen of People Repellent on the back of his neck and on his arms. Mosquitoes followed, whining around his ears before dipping their beaks into their newfound nirvana.

They itched, and he was surprised by just how many flying insects were living in his house, but he also understood what was happening with perfect clarity. He went outside and walked slowly down the sidewalk, heading towards his girlfriend's house just a few blocks away. A thousand thousand more insects joined their brethren on his flesh. His body became a living block party for the local gnats. Moths landed on his eyelids. Honeybees buzzed and nuzzled into his belt line. And people quickly got out of his way.

He was a living coat of writhing wrigglers when he rang her doorbell, waiting to see what kind of person she'd turn out to be. Beneath a mitten of mites, he still clutched the spray bottle in a free hand, which he held behind his back like a lover's bouquet.

Fortune Cookie: A Parable

The waiter brought us our check on a little silver tray, bowing while politely setting it beside my plate. Atop the scribbled paper were two fortune cookies, wrapped in wax paper, which suggested they were homemade.

"Oooh," Paul said from across the table, reaching out.

I playfully slapped his hand away. "I already told you, Paul. Dinner's on me."

He kept his hand wavering in the air. "That doesn't mean you get all the cookies." He went for the tray again.

I moved it out of his reach—which was fairly easy because he was sloshed on pear wine. "It doesn't work that way," I said, waiting for him to put his hand back down.

He lifted a shoulder and sneered in a childish taunt, then picked up his glass instead, slurping down what remained in it. "Vine," he said, slurring the F.

"You have to follow protocols with these things. You're not supposed to just grab your own fortune like that. Fate is handed to you." I picked up the tray. "So I serve you yours, and you serve me mine." I slid the bill out from under the cookies the way a magician pulls the tablecloth out from under a dinner set. Then I presented him with the cookies on the platter. "Take."

He picked the cookie on the left—going for the bigger one—and immediately unwrapped its wax paper purse, not bothering to take the tray from my hand and serve me mine.

I set the platter down and slid it across the table, next to the black porcelain plates that had earlier cradled his meal.

"Oh, this is a big one," he said, holding the cookie in front of his face, and then pinching one end with his free hand. He snapped it crisply in half, with a few small pieces tinkling the porcelain below.

He read it aloud: "There's nothing more dangerous than an idea if it's the only one you have."

"So true..."

"In bed!" he shouted, then laughed in a way that was clearly intended to get the other patrons in the restaurant to join in on the joke.

They uncomfortably tried to ignore him.

I didn't have that luxury. "Okay, my turn..." I signaled at the remaining cookie by his dinner plate.

Paul was clueless. "Wait, I don't get it. I thought fortunes were supposed to predict the future." He scrutinized the tiny ribbon of paper, his lips moving as he whispered it over again to himself, as if double-checking the message. Then he lifted an eyebrow as he repeated it again, as loud as a patron complaining about the food. "This just insults me with a platitude." He looked at me. "I want to know what the future holds. Give me a new one."

He moved to pick up the cookie I was waiting on. I lunged and saved it from his grasp. He frowned.

"Paul," I said with a smile, enjoying the fact that he wasn't getting what he wanted. "Every fortune cookie does tell the future in its own way. Maybe it's a warning about some idea you will have in the future...or a mystical comment from the beyond about something you're working on right now." I leaned over my own cookie and decided that I might as well just eat it, fate or not.

He frowned, unable to shake his frustration. He looked around the room as if to summon the waiter, then his gaze fell on me, fondling the free cookie. "I feel cheated!"

"Just think about it," I said, unwrapping the wax paper, eager to get a sugar boost.

Then he gurgled. I looked up.

His chest cavity pushed forward like a rooster's as his neck went limp. I thought he might be having a heart attack, but then there was an unholy sound of bones popping skin as his ribcage buckled. It was as if his body had been snapped in half, clutched in the fist of an unseen giant.

I shot out of my chair, moving to help him—but it was too late. He fell to the floor.

In halves. Impossibly, one side of Paul's body slumped to the left and the other fell to the right at exactly the same time. It wasn't until the place where his shoulders should have been fell to the chair seat and his clothes spilled open that I realized: he had somehow broken in half.

Just like his fortune cookie.

I dropped the cookie I was clutching.

And then I, too, fell to the floor.

Brian Keene Must Die

"And then his face caved in."

Brian Keene leaned back in his rickety old chair and evaluated the sentence. The whole book had led up to that one line, and it was a damned good one. He couldn't think of a better way to end his 42nd novel.

But he could think of a better way to end the night. He walked across his office, opened a file drawer labeled "research" and pushed aside a hanging folder of old comic books, till he found what he thought might still be hidden there, from many years ago. His fingers found the hockey puck-sized canister and he chuckled to himself as he pulled it out.

"Good old Kodiak," he said, tapping the green can of snuff against his thigh. He went outside and enjoyed the night moon. The crickets. The hum of the world.

And he ran his finger around the rim of his ancient can of Kodiak chewing tobacco. The one he hid in a drawer many, many novels ago—when he had a full head of hair and enough spunk left in him to try to kick the habit. He'd hidden the chew in his files "just in case" he wouldn't be able to endure the withdrawals. Instead, he'd gotten so drunk on Knob Creek that night he'd blacked out and forgotten it was there. It sat there for years—at least fifteen—and—aside from his nightly pull from a flask of Knob Creek—most of his addictions were long behind him. He'd totally forgotten the can of snuff was in the drawer until just a moment ago, when he wrote those final words to *The Lowering* and somehow it tripped a lightswitch on in the closet of his memories and he instantly remembered it.

He took a whiff of the can, like a wine critic sniffing a cork. Fifteen years old, but it smelt great, and memories of his snuff days came flooding back to him. It didn't smell like chewing tobacco at all. More like a cross between fermented grapes and graveyard earth. The fact that it was still smelly at all surprised him, but then again, very little surprised him now that he was in his late 70s. He gently tapped a finger on the mound of black leaves and its tar stuck to the pads of his fingers.

He rubbed the leaves between them and the tobacco leaves crisped into powder, but left a minty residue on his fingertips, which he sniffed one more time to check his senses. It smelled tasty. Chewable.

"Screw it," he said and took the flask out of his back pocket. He poured Knob Creek all over the stuff to kill any bugs that might have grown inside. Surely something had grown in the festering can over the years, no? But maybe the can fermented the stuff like whiskey and was sealed so well that chewing it would be like drinking ancient wine. Who knew? So he took a healthy pinch and balled it up and packed it between his cheek and gum, just like he used to do it in the old days: testing the capacity of his cheek by pushing it down firmly with his tongue.

It didn't taste rancid at all. It tasted better than he even remembered Kodiak ever tasting. Saliva pooled in his mouth and he spit at a crumpled Budweiser can on the grass nearby, which made a metallic "pop" when his spit hit it, like he'd shot it with a pistol.

He sat on his steps and wished he had one of those great ornate spittoons from the old west. He spit again, and felt like Josey Wales when the can not only "popped" but leapt up in the air from the impact. He watched the blackened spit crawl down the BUD label, glimmering in the moonlight, leaves of old Kodiak sticking to the aluminum.

In fact, the moonlight glimmer of his spit seemed too familiar. The drool was too white. It reminded him of something he couldn't quite place.

He swirled more spit around in his mouth. The chew was beginning to sting a little, to sour his gum tissue up. Almost as though the "pinch" were pinching back. He could feel the stems poking him.

He spit again, to get some of it out of his mouth.

It pinged the can like a bullet, and it rattled across the grass, smeary with his saliva.

And the he saw what was so shiny in the spittle.

It wasn't the shine of the moon. It was a different kind of whiteness. At first he thought it might be paint on the tin can, flecking off from impact of his sharply shot acidic spit. He stood, picked up the can, and held it up to the moon to get a better look.

And he saw teeth. Little tiny teeth.

And he knew that the pinch in his lip was not old stem and acidic tobacco at all, but the manic chewing of those tiny teeth—a least a hundred of them. Ancient microbial teeth, mature and angry from being locked inside the Kodiac can over all those many years. He had to laugh, as the image of microscopic little Kodiac bears popped into his unflinching dark imagination: tiny grizzlies, gnashing their muzzles into the field of pink tissue, tearing bloody chunks of the stuff out with a snap of the neck and the claw of their heavy feet. It seemed preposterous, and the wounds would surely be minimal, since this was all in the close-up magnification of his mind. But the image wouldn't go away and he could feel the chewing tobacco chewing and it began to make him more than a little uncomfortable, so he tried to probe the wad out with his tongue.

But it wouldn't let go. The wad of Kodiak kept chewing and held firm, gripping the pink muscle with its nasty claws and it wouldn't let go no matter how hard he tried to plunge and spit it out...and the monstrous teeth gnashed and clawed and the orgy of writhing little animals—not bears at all—not even animals of this world—but no less grizzly, and no less hungry—pulled the bolus of themselves down into his gullet...and as he choked and snortled and fell to the ground beside the beer can, he could feel them grinding their way down his throat, eating him inside out, eating right through his larynx, and the blood was spewing both up and down now—he could feel it spritzing from a torn artery and shooting against the walls of his esophagus, streaming up his windpipe and into his nasal cavity while also flooding down into his lungs, and he needed air, he needed air, and he tried to scream for help but his larynx was gone and the motion of his jaw just unhinged what was left of his lock on life. And the chewing tobacco chewed. It chewed its way into his ribcage, then his stomach lining, where it found the whiskey flavor it hungered for.

And then his face caved in.

[Note: *Yes, the protagonist of this story is inspired by the real horror author, Briane Keene. This story was one of several online "killings" of Keene, which he sadistically invited from horror writers everywhere as a sort of "charitable theme anthology" online, to call attention to the financial need for donations to the Shirley Jackson Award. You can still donate at* http://www.shirleyjacksonawards.org]

Introducing MyBlade

Thank you for coming out tonight, to this momentous occasion. I'm here to introduce you to a breakthrough technology, one that will change the very way you live your life.

It's called MyBlade.

And this fantastic device is literally cutting edge.

MyBlade is the world's first electronic knife. You heard me right. This is no mere "electric" knife intended to simply carve your way through a tough turkey. It can do that, true, but no, MyBlade is not electric. It is *electronic*. Inside its handle is a 3.4gHz microcomputer with 8 Gigabytes of memory, interfacing directly with a 16-inch stainless steel surgical-quality blade.

MyBlade will entirely change the way you slice, dice, chop and fillet.

Let me tell you all about it.

The "brain" of MyBlade allows you to set the slicing speed at just the right level—from a slow-saw to a rapid slice that would put even a chainsaw to shame. I'm talking up to 30,000 slices per second, more than the naked eye can see, even up close.

It heats or cools the steel to a temperature you select—or it can recommend just the right level of heat for what it's about to cut. In fact, MyBlade is the first cutting instrument to actually cook the very meat it slices, as it slices it!

You heard me right. No need for an oven. You can make yourself a hot pot roast sandwich with raw beef. And if you happen to somehow cut yourself or someone else, you won't need to worry about dialing 911. The wound will instantly be cauterized!

But yes, even if you still want to dial 911, it can do that for you, too. Did I mention that MyBlade is wireless? And networked? Indeed, it is online and can be used as a phone, a pager, a web browser, and an IM communication center.

But it's still, ultimately, a knife. The greatest knife ever invented. It will cut on demand or your money back.

It's self-cleaning and self-oiling. MyBlade even automatically detects if its edges are dull—and it self-sharpens while it rests in its charging bay.

It can be voice-activated. It can be remote controlled, or operated with an internet browser from your office. Prepare your dinner while you're still at work!

And you can listen to over 1000 songs while you chop, sheer... or even shave!

Amazed?

You've only seen a small part of what MyBlade can do. I haven't even mentioned its main breakthrough new technology, one only made possible by the invention of something so amazing as MyBlade.

Sonic slicing. And sonic slicing will revolutionize the way you literally make cuts.

The speed of MyBlade is so fast that its subsonic frequencies literally spread the molecules that surround it.

We could have stopped there, but we didn't.

MyBlade also records sounds while it slices, saving unique sonic footprints that only MyBlade itself can hear. This is cutting up close, closer than it's ever been before. Press the silver button on its grip, and you can save every chop, hack, and stab you make to the copious mp3 storage drive built inside its form-fitting handle.

Cut a sandwich or cut a track—the choice is yours. It is the first musical instrument of its kind, and butchers around the world have already begun composing some amazing new music. You can hear them—and join them by sharing your own cuts—online at the knife's hone page.

Did I say hone page? I meant home page. And MyBlade logs on instantly, BladeCasting to the world.

Still not sold?

Well, let me demonstrate. Here, put these MyPhones in your ears.

Now give me your arm.

Don't worry. MyBlade cauterizes. And trust me, it's faster than you'll believe.

That's right, go ahead and sing along. We're BladeCasting live. And it's my arm now.

Pink Flamingos

You lift the puffy creature and titter when its feathers tickle the underside of your chin. You hug it tight as the bird's spindly legs kick madly around your waist and its ugly bill clacks dangerously close to your neck.

You carry the awkward bird to your front yard and slam it down onto the metal post that awaits it—impaling the fat fowl in a flurry of feathers and blood—its manic beak snapping wildly at your arms as you back away. It never protests with a caw or a squeak; it simply kicks and smacks its beak, its cartilaginous appendages smacking against one another like the limbs of some unearthly crustacean. The flamingo's head bobs on its lanky neck like a boxer's as it tries to decide whether to attack you or to flutter away, as if unaware of the immobility that underpins this uncertainty.

Its eyes pierce into you as the bird shudders on its pole, molting enough feathers in the process to cover the bloody puddle beneath it. Eventually, the gravity of its skull becomes too much for the lanky neck to bear and the head falls down with all the impotency of a garden hose, emptied of water.

You admire its graceful flight from life.

You admire its beautiful new stature.

You hope your neighbors will appreciate your new Halloween decoration.

But you're not certain. They missed the dead midget standing in your garden last year, after all.

Election Day Alarm: A Parable

The brassy horn blows, stirring him from slumber. Not a horn, he realizes as he opens his eyes—an electronic drone, the tone on his "gentle wake" alarm clock that rises a notch up in volume every ten seconds until the sleeper turns it off. He lifts his heavy eyelids and confronts the clock face. 6:56 am. Too early. He hates this whining clock. Its siren creeps on him. Its soft tone deceives him.

He's not sure if he wants to get out of bed yet. He watches the digits on the clock—the boxy numbers burning like three blurry gold bars into his eyes. He hesitates to turn the alarm off. Doesn't want to acknowledge the coming day. But he doesn't want to snooze, either. Politics is a tough game, and he's not done with it yet. Even if he wins today's election, he'll have to make a lot of changes. Not sure he wants to. Not sure the time is right. Not sure of anything. It's all in the hands of those who cast the votes, anyway.

6:56. The horn blares.

The waiting, he thinks, is unbearable. Always is. His wife finally groans beside him, tossing covers. He wonders if he's just awakened the new first lady or the wife of yet another has-been.

The clock finally turns the next digit with an audible click. He presses the button. Silence. He gets up and puts on his fancy suit.

The numbers on the clock read 6:66.

You're Not Getting Sleepy

You're not getting sleepy. Why not? I've tried every trick in the hypnotist's handbook. From the swinging gold watch to the spinning spiral top to the repetitious patterning of my deep, monotone voice... and nothing works.

How dare you test my mental dominance? I have degrees in parapsychology and television advertising. I have studied ancient unbound manuscripts in libraries that are kept secret from even the real magicians, like Doug Henning. But I have gone farther into the mysteries of the mind than most; there is no hypnotic method I have not mastered. I have memorized trade secrets from how-to books by used car salesmen and I know all the tricks from every "How to Get a Person in Bed" book ever published. Yet you seem impenetrable to every mind-bending technique.

You. You think you're so smart. You believe that no one can bend your free will, except, perhaps, brain surgeons who know how to trigger reactions by prodding the scarlet sponge with their cold instruments. Uncivil brutes! I can manipulate your nerve endings without even touching flesh. I can seduce you with my eyes in a stare that puts Bela Lugosi to shame. I can lull you into a waking dream state with my voice in a way that makes nursing mothers and day care workers jealous. When I pull on your aura with my electric fingers, you will feel me in every way. I can seduce your optic nerves into seeing things that aren't there—indeed, Hollywood wishes they could market me. When it comes to the trance state, I'm more potent than any pill or history book. My methods of persuasion require no technology. My power is genuine.

So why do you still resist? Why do you not succumb to my charm?

Don't you understand?

I will not simply put you to sleep. I will make you dream that which is not possible within your puny perception of the world.

But still you resist.

I will not make you cockle-doodle-doo like a chicken whilst

flopping your elbows. I will serve you a fricassee of air that you can taste and swallow and actually feel hot in your gullet. In fact, I could even get you to cannibalize other people who I have transformed into a chicken, and relish the taste of their meat. Yes, my powers are that strong.

But still you resist!

Enough.

Look into my eyes. Deeply. See the vast expanse of the universe—the galaxies of sparkling stars, spiraling into the center of two blacker-than-black black holes. Feel them pulling you into their vacuum, gently—like a raft of driftwood pulling slowly away from shore. Feel the genuine release of your worries as you cascade around the swirling shower of light. Your mind is free from the bindings of your heavy body. Your eyelids are losing their power as you swirl in the vortex of my abyss. Freedom waits around every turn and twist. You are getting sleepy, sleepy....

When I snap my fingers, you will believe that this job interview was the best you have ever conducted. You will not only want to hire me, you will give me the maximum salary and benefits and turn the other way when I seduce secretaries and charm accountants and beat the boss at golf.

One. Two....

Oh, come on! Please?

Sprayers

I dragged myself out of bed and into the bathroom. I was ritually brushing my teeth, ritually foaming at the mouth in the mirror, ritually bored. But then the foam turned pink with blood and I knew it was the blood from my dreams, the blood I'd slurped from a skunk's neck like a vampire in my black-and-white dreams, the blood that tasted like paprika and cloves on my tongue as the sour musky oil jetted out of the skunk's ass, streaming all the way over to a nearby tree for a good two seconds before trickling down to just a quivering rivulet that poured over the back of my hand, the hand that broke the skunk's spine as my teeth sunk in around the cord at its neck. Kneeling in the earthy loam of my dream, I was a skunk vampire on all fours, my widow's peak black as oil, my hair slicked back on my head and freaked with broad white lines as I gnawed into the throat of the animal I'd just murdered, my beard lapping against the skunk's wet fur like a bloody paintbrush. I used the paintbrush to change the skunk's white lines to red. I looked at the mirror and realized I was brushing my teeth with an electric razor, before I used the razor to paintbrush away the beard. I smiled with bloody gums and neglected to use deodorant as I got dressed and headed to my job, spraying fragrance samples on interested passers-by at the shopping mall.

Silence

The sun of the Nevada desert bakes the steaming wreckage.
Blood boils on the tarmac beneath two minivans.
A black vulture circles above, then descends.

All is silent, save for a fading radiator hiss.
Fluids sizzling on hot tar.
And a baby's cry.

The vulture pecks first
into the shattered eye socket of father,
sprawled on the hood.
Then the mother's arm, somewhere
beside her corpse in the front seat.

The baby's cry from the back of the car
annoys the munching vulture,
who assesses the child's immobility
before fluttering over to the other van
to sort through the pickings.

The bird finds an open rib cage,
a wet container of meat.
It noses aside the torn uniform shirt
with an Atomic symbol on its pocket,
before stabbing its beak
full bore into the driver's diseased lungs.

The baby in the family van cries for its mother.
The vulture can ignore its squealing no longer.

It flutters back to the first van
and perches on a bloody headrest,
talons clutching brain and brown vinyl.

The baby cries, eyes squinched, oblivious.

The vulture hops carefully
to the plastic edge of the child seat.
It eyeballs the stained straps.
It cocks its mangy head to one side
while watching the child's small lips
quivering with pain.

The vulture sidles over and perches above
the baby's soft, bruised head.
Its wings rustle.
A veiny, purple hand slides out
from the feathery pits at its side,
dripping moist with slime.

The vulture leans forward
and muffles the noise of its prey.

All is silent, save for a fading radiator hiss.
Fluids sizzling on hot tar.
And soon the smacking of mutant beak.

BLATHERING LISTS

Selections from The Goreletter

"Blather" is the name of the opening essay in each issue of my e-newsletter, The Goreletter, where anything goes. Sometimes I'll post a thinkpiece about some topic related to the horror genre (in one issue, I made up a series of "Monster Mashes I'd Like to See" that included "Hannibal Lector vs. the Mummy" and "Norman Bates vs. Norman Bates"); at other times, I'll write essays on some element of everyday life worthy of reflection through the lens of horror (such as my probing examination of the creepy images of animals on pet food packages or my musing over the disgusting nature of fingernails); and sometimes I'll just make up sick and wacky lists, often in the vein of articles I remember from the old *MAD* magazine.

The lists are my favorite to write. They're like poetry, and I often read from them at live performances. And since you're probably inclined to like such things, I'm including my favorites here, as a sampler of my newsletter, for your enjoyment.

13 Furnishings You'll NEVER Find at IKEA

BAGEMUP
Mob Hit Throw Rug with Latex Backing

GNUCKS
Knucklebone Beaded Curtain

HOOGAFLOOF
Neck Pillow Stuffed with Ukrainian Owl Eyes

NOZZOIKS
Teflon Glove for Throwing Electric Chair Switches

JYMJONZ
Paper Cup Dispenser

SMÊGMAR
Bordello Mattress Liner

STYNXEE
Swedish Pine Urinal Disc

SLAZISUZI
Saw Blade Turntable Appetizer Tray

BRÅNZ
Chrome Cannibal Serving Bowl with Designer Drip Saucer

OFFTAPOTTER
Stuffed Otter's Head Toilet Brush

LILCOUGHIN
Children's Storage Unit

BETÎPAJ
Beechwood Rotating Whip Rack with Emergency First Aid
Kit

BLÜGH:
Envelope Moistener/Spittoon

Return of the Son of Pride and Prejudice and Zombies

Cthulhu the Obscure
A Connecticut Devil in King Arthur's Inferno
The Golden Bowl of Blood
The Isle of Dr. Moreau and Mr. Hyde
As I Lay Resurrecting
Creature from the Walden Pond
Of Mice and Tentacles
A Midsummer Night's Scream
Jane Weyrewolf
Oedipus Rex: The Boy With the X-Ray Eyes
Uncle Tom's Cannibal Cabin
A Poison Clockwork Orange
Rabid Animal Farm
Lord of the Giant Flies
Clone King Richard the Thirtieth
A Morgue of One's Own

Weird Juice

Stabble
Fungalberry
Kiweird Cocktail
Poisonberry
Phlegmonaid (With Extra Pulp)

Embalmigranate
Bashin' Berry
Scabapple
Scrape Juice
Angerine

Spineapple
Strango
Slaughtermelon Smoothie
Crampelope
Slimeade

Neck Nectar
Horrange
Slitrus Lime
Gaspberry
Upchuck Cherry

Slopical Punch
Scarfruit
Granbury
Scarrot
Leech

Classic Car Accident Ad Slogans

Have You Driven A F*rd Over A Stroller Lately?
This Is Your Late Father's *ldsmobile.
V*lvo. For Life Support.
Killt F*rd Slough.
Ch*vy. The Last Heartbeat Of America.
Chummer—Like Nothing Else!
Ponti*c. We Are Driving Excrement.
Grab Life By The Horns. That Won't Stop Honking.
Sa*b. Move Your Mind. Off My Lap.
B*W. The Ultimate Chicken Machine.
V*lkswagon. Drivers Haunted.
Juice In Engineering. *udi.
C*dillac. When You Turn Your Car Off, Does It Return The Favor?
Unlike Any Other. Mortcedez Endz.
B*ick. Drive Beautiful. Into Crowds.
The All New Ch*vy. Built To Last Breath.
H*nda. The Power Of Screams.
S*turn. Like Always. Like Never Before. Like Rotten Haggis.
L*coln. Reach Higher. We're Sinking.
I Hate What You Did To Me—T*yota!
Tahrvernoggin!

Why it Sucks to be a Cyclops

The giant monocle seldom looks flattering.

The forehead horn is completely worthless. It just gets in the way, actually.

The loss of depth perception makes it hard to know just where to bite when feasting on live meat.

No one gets it when you wink at them.

The eye chart at the optometrist's office is really an "eyes chart." Not that you can read. But still.

The insensitive slurs from the two-eyed community ("myopic," "short-sighted," etc.) are never-ending.

Only Siamese twins get to look cross-eyed.

The giant single eyeball only assists the archer's aim.

The pirate's patch fools no one.

Cartoons have filled the children you eat with all sort of false assumptions about how you do so. (However, this can be a benefit, if you have the right Cyclopean attitude).

If you lose a contact, you're doomed.

The Encyclopedia has been replaced by the Wikipedia.

Proverbs for Monsters

Slime never feels slimy to slime.
Bark all you like, the man in the moon has no ears.
Biting off the head silences the victim. But it is the feet that will
    stop them from running away.
Beware of things that go bump in the day.
Man, like monster, also has sharp teeth.
Those who most shun garlic, often most enjoyed it in their youth.
The sleep of madness brings forth humanity.
Wear gold jewelry. When silver is in fashion, wear even more of it.
Like a stake through the heart, so is the love of the clergy.
A man eating plant will even swallow a vegetarian, when hungry.
A garbled threat is but a spell cast by an illiterate witch.
An infant vampire bites hardest.
Even werewolves shave during the day.
It is not your tentacles, but the acid that drips from them,
    that frightens your prey.
Those who fear the sun too soon often awaken before sundown.
One can catch a good human with a bad hamburger.
Holy water stings but a neck bite is forever.
Nothing is more stupid than an exposed brain.
Fortune favors the cleaver.

Halloween Costumes I Wish
I Would Have Seen

Pushpinhead
Sumo Uncle Fester
The SlimJim Reaper
Shattered Stunt Man Skeleton
Apple Sauce
Osama Been Rotting
Transvestite "Double-Yuh"
Fixed Lethargic Cat
Drawn and Quartered Gladiator
Suicidal Van Helsing
Quivering Giblets in Blood Gravy
Zombie Homeless Man (with "Will Work for Brains" sign)
My Very Own Doppelganger
Plaque

Ways in Which Moving is Like Death

Good friends do heavy lifting. They probably will drink and eat afterwards.

Your apartment is up for grabs.

Sadly, you will leave things behind. But more of it will end up in the trash than you imagined possible.

On the day of departure, you won't be able to say goodbye to everyone you'd hoped to.

Some of your friends will have trouble saying goodbye for the first time since you've known them.

Your past becomes legend far too quickly. Even the secret stuff.

You can't take it with you. I'm referring, of course, to that thing some jerk borrowed and never returned. Now it's really gone.

Your eating and showering habits are altered and you will resent this.

Your new address is uncertain.

Your neighbors stink.

A Casebook of Criticism

Literary Critics on the Gorelets Experiment

Change Thy Shape: The Metamorphoses of Horror

by Lawrence C. Connolly

Consider Marlowe's *Doctor Faustus*.

The play begins with Faustus contemplating his books: Aristotle's *Analytics*, Jerome's *Bible*, Galen's discourses on medicine. The works have been the center of his world, but now he wants new diversions. For help, he turns to Mephistopheles.

Enter the prototype of the digital-age writer. While Aristotle and Galen are stuck in their books, Mephistopheles travels through the ether, responding to Faustus' call. Faustus, however, isn't sold on the initial package. It isn't quite what he had in mind. "I charge thee to return and change thy shape," he says, and Mephistopheles complies, repackages himself, and gains a soul.

To be sure, disenchantment with books and shape-changing are only part of the Faustus story, but for our discussion, let us consider Act I, the image of a reader in search of new diversions. Is it worth the effort to reach out to such an audience, and what is to be done with these souls, once their attention has been won? Most of all, what is at stake and what is to be gained?

By way of answers, let us examine the shape-changing works of a writer who frequently moves beyond paper and ink, through the ether, and into a variety of readily accessible shapes and packages. Our discussion will center on two major collections (one poetry, the other prose) and the writer behind them.

Michael A. Arnzen began using computer technology to package his work in 1991, when he employed a rudimentary form of desktop publishing to produce a 42-page chapbook entitled *Chew and Other Ruminations*. Published under (and launching) his own imprint, Mastication Publications, the book featured illustrations from five artists whose work had been appearing alongside his in various small-press magazines. These were the early days of PageMaker, but with the cost of software and the hardware to run it beyond the reach of his student finances, Arnzen made do with a Brother word processor and help from artist Renate Müller, who collaborated with Arnzen to create a professional-looking design at a fraction of what the book would have cost using state-of-the-art computing. Modest success followed. According to Arnzen:

> I basically sold it to small press outlets, got it reviewed in small genre and/or "little" mags, and used it to have something to sell (and giveaway) at cons. Like Thomas Paine, I guess, only more like Thomas Pain. (Arnzen, "Re: Questions")

The pun on Paine (Arnzen might say 'pun of pain') is an intriguing reminder that, as Bertrand Russell tells us, the right man will arrive at the right time to change history. Charles Fort, referring to such a moment as "steam-engine-time," points out that the ingredients of profound change often lie unnoticed until someone is capable of recognizing their significance (34). This is a good point to keep in mind, for in 1991, as Arnzen and Müller were employing primitive computer technology to publish *Chew*, other more dramatic opportunities were taking shape in the world of digital communication. One of these was the release of a public Internet service called the World Wide Web (Berners-Lee). The other was the emergence of pen-based or "pen-top" computing that allowed the general user to write rather than key data and text onto a computer screen (Reinhardt). Both would soon provide Arnzen with the means of moving beyond the printed page and into the as yet undeveloped realm of digital communication.

Arnzen began exploring the Internet's possibilities while attending graduate school at the University of Oregon. His first Internet creation, *Arnzen's Arbor Vitae* (launched in the mid-90s), was one of the first websites devoted to horror, and by working on it Arnzen developed the skills needed to start *Gorelets*—a subscription-based poetry project in 2001—at http://gorelets.com

Initially, the project was intended to provide readers with short poems that could be read on handheld PDA readers. He was certainly not the first to make literature available for such devices, but while others publishers such as NuvoMedia,

SoftBook and a variety of Web-based companies were charging readers for longer material that was already available in print (Hillesund), Arnzen set about producing a series of original short poems, which he called "gorelets," written specially to fit on the screen of a PDA reader, no scrolling required. As Arnzen tells it:

> I realized that e-books were everywhere, but nowhere was poetry. And poetry just seemed to fit the screen better than long, eternally scrolling documents written for print rather than pixels. (Arnzen, "Introduction", 9)

But what would readers pay for these poems? Major publishers were asking the same question about their ebook novels, and it was becoming increasingly evident that some readers were reluctant to pay printed-book prices for digital editions. According to M.J. Rose, best-selling author of *Lip Service* (2001), "People are much more willing to read on the desktop when it doesn't cost them a lot" (Mayfield), and in early 2001, Pocket Books tested this proposition by offering digital editions of two of Rose's titles for $4.95, nine dollars less than their print counterparts. Concurrently, Del Rey offered the ebook edition of its *Star Wars* title *Darth Maul: Saboteur* for $1.99 (Mayfield). Seeing the writing on the screen, Arnzen offered his gorelet subscriptions for free.

For a year, starting in August 2001, a new gorelet poem appeared each week. Readers could download each work directly from Gorelets.com, or subscribers could have them hotsynched directly to their handheld PDAs. Some readers were delighted, with as many as 1,000 visitors dropping by the website each month during the year that the gorelet downloads were available (Arnzen, "Personal Interview"). Others were unimpressed, as was one skeptic at Geek.com who felt that the project seemed to be designed for PDA users who would download "any old toss—so long as it's PDA-centric" ("Horror Author"). But the beauty of the little poems was that they were not "PDA-centric," for even as PDA users were downloading them for handheld readers, others were opting to receive print editions—in the form of postcards.

Postcard publishing is not a new idea in fantastic literature. Arthur C. Clarke tells the story of British editor George Hay, who in the mid-1970s had

the ingenious idea of putting out a complete science fiction
story on a postcard—together with a stamp-sized photo of
the author. Fans would, he believed, buy these in hundreds
to mail out to their friends. (Clarke 49)

Hay's plan never got off the ground. In spite of his acquisition of new short-
short stories by the likes of Clarke and Asimov, the postcards were never
published, leading Clarke to speculate that "probably the rising cost of
postage killed the scheme" (Clarke 49).

Clarke's ironic comment underscores one of the economic realities of print
publishing, and Arnzen was going to need an efficient and economical means of
printing and distributing his gorelet postcards if his plan was going to succeed.
Fortunately, the means were available in the form of an Internet service called
AmazingMail, whose mission was to provide an "economical and convenient way
to send […] postcards directly from your computer to anyone in the world via US
Mail" ("Who Are We"). With the help of *Chew* artist Renate Müller (now Renate
Arnzen), who provided him with a crash course in the use of Paint Shop Pro, Arnzen
created original illustrations for the fronts of the cards and AmazingMail took care
of production and distribution. Though not free (Arnzen was charging $13 for a
base subscription of a dozen postcards, $78 for a full run of 52), subscriptions came
with some value-added features that helped justify purchasing what some readers
were receiving in the form of free downloads. One of those features involved
password-protected access to an online archive of the full run of gorelet poems.
With this service, late subscribers could read digital copies of the poems they had
missed. In addition, there was a second feature that served to elevate the series
to limited-edition status. The fifth card in every subscription was a special signed
edition that Arnzen printed and mailed on his own (rather than processing through
AmazingMail). Thus, whereas the PDA versions provided fleeting diversions for
readers on the move, the postcard series offered signed *objets d'art* for collectors.

After the PDA and postcard editions completed their runs in August
2002, all of the poems and many of the Paint Shop images were collected in

a chapbook edition entitled *Gorelets: Unpleasant Poems* (2003). Thus, within two years, Arnzen had made each gorelet available in three different forms, each for a different kind of reader. But the metamorphoses would not end there. Well before the release of the Fairwood Press edition, Arnzen was already at work developing a fourth incarnation that would prove to be the most subversive of them all, one that appealed not to readers but to writers, puzzle solvers and game players. For this new format, Arnzen disassembled the poems, reducing them to a collection of random words, which he presented as digital magnets on a cyber-refrigerator that he created using JavaScript. Visitors to Gorelets.com were invited to arrange the words to create poems of their own. The would-be poets could then post their creations in a frame labeled "Moldy Cheese: Poems from The Refrigerator of the Damned."

With "The Refrigerator of the Damned" (alternately titled "The Damned Fridge") Arnzen claims he was confronting his own fear of making his original work available in digital form. What if subscribers began modifying the poems, creating variations that they then passed off as their own work? As Arnzen tells it, "I took the fear I had of people using my stuff and turned it into The Refrigerator of the Damned" (Arnzen, "Personal Interview"). The experiment proved successful, soon capturing the attention of editor Peggy Jo Shumate at Double Dragon Publishing, who asked writers to generate poems using "The Damned Fridge" and submit them to a hardback poetry collection entitled *Cemetery Poets* (2003). Published the same year as *Gorelets: Unpleasant Poems*, the reshaped gorelets in *Cemetery Poets* are yet another shape-change for the transmutable gorelets. But the metamorphosis doesn't end there, for by year's end Double Dragon also released a newly expanded version of the Fairwood Press edition as an ebook. Here, two years after Arnzen began scribbling them with his digital stylus, the poems returned to their original format, pixels on handheld readers and computer screens.

More than just an intriguing experiment, the various manifestations of Gorelets attracted readers and recognition that Arnzen would not have had if he had limited himself to traditional print publication. Moreover, given the short shelf-life of mass-market paperbacks, even an award-winning novel such as Arnzen's *Grave Markings* (1994) will do little to garner continued recognition in today's marketplace. In an era when the print version of an original novel is given barely a month to prove itself before being stripped and tossed in the dumpster, any undertaking that garners a Stoker nomination (for the Fairwood edition), coverage in non-genre publications as diverse as *Wired News* and *Pittsburgh City Paper*, and about 1,000 Internet hits a month would seem to be worth the effort. Indeed, it is worth noting that a number of those hits and downloads come from outside the traditional audience for horror and poetry, readers drawn in by online press releases posted for PDA users (Arnzen, "New Media Horror"). In the long term, Arnzen hopes that these new readers, some of whom have become interested enough in what he is doing to offer voluntary contributions to the effort, will also become readers of his more traditional work, such as his novels, which, as of this writing, are only available in print editions (Arnzen, "Comments").

By the time Fairwood Press was readying the print edition of his ultra-short poems, Arnzen was already at work on *100 Jolts: Shockingly Short Stories* (2004). A Stoker finalist, the book earned raves from readers at Amazon.com and from critics at the usual genre-related websites. The book is currently available in trade paperback and ebook editions, but an attempt to make the individual stories available through a new venue that Arnzen called the "Sickolodeon" met with some initial problems.

Although he had made his short-short poems available as free downloads, Arnzen felt that readers should pay something for digital copies of the longer works in *100 Jolts*. Recalling how early filmmakers distributed their work in Nickelodeons, Arnzen devised a delivery system called the "Sickolodeon," through which readers could pay to access individual stories. At the heart of this plan was an Internet company called BitPass.com.

Founded in December 2002 with the help of comic artist Scott McCloud, BitPass was initially an online market through which comic artists sold their creations. It soon expanded to offer a variety of content (music, films, graphics, texts and even schematic diagrams for patented inventions) for nominal charges called micropayments.

The micropayment plan is simple. After opening a BitPass account (which provides the customer with an Internet credit card), a member can begin purchasing small-ticket content from over 3,000 participating merchants ("BitPass Appoints"). The customer's account is then debited in small increments for each selection. Arnzen saw the service as an opportunity to make individual stories from *100 Jolts* available for nominal fees. Alas, there were problems. In early February 2006, people attempting to access the "Sickolodeon" through Gorelets.com were presented with a notice stating that the Sickolodeon was "under reconstruction" (Arnzen, "The Sickolodeon"). The problem, according to Arnzen, resulted from recent changes that BitPass had done to its programming code. To correct the problem and bring Sickolodeon back on line, Arnzen would need to spend some time rewriting his program. Today, it seems, it is not enough to be skilled at writing poetry and prose. It also helps to be fluent in HTML. Moreover, it also helps to have an Internet service provider capable of handling the necessary programming language. At the moment, Arnzen indicates that he is at the mercy of his ISP, which he reports "doesn't seem to be quite "ready" for the programming language BitPass is using" (Arnzen, "Comments").

Fortunately, problems with the "Sickolodeon" have not marked the end of the *100 Jolts* metamorphosis. Filmmaker Jim Minton has taken some of the stories (along with a number of Arnzen's *Gorelets* and works from various chapbooks) and adapted them for a film entitled *Exquisite Corpse* (2006). Minton, a filmmaker who has worked in the entertainment industry for 25 years, lined up a roster of international filmmakers to direct the individual segments of the film. Arnzen, who signed on for a straight percentage, says that Minton planned "to release a version of the film (probably an extended excerpt) on the Independent Film Channel website (ifilm.com)" (Arnzen, "Comments"). Beyond that, one can only speculate what the creator of *Gorelets*, *The Refrigerator of the Damned*, and the 'Sickolodeon' might do once he has access to a series of short digital films based on his stories.

Although *Gorelets* and *100 Jolts* demonstrate Arnzen's ability to take the written word beyond the traditional realms of ink and paper, no discussion of such endeavors would be complete without mention of his Bram Stoker Award-winning email newsletter, "The Goreletter."

Launched the month after the last gorelet was hotsynched to a subscriber's PDA, "The Goreletter" was designed as yet another way to keep in touch with readers. The Goreletter continues to provide a blend of news, commentary and humor to a growing list of subscribers. It also keeps readers posted regarding changes and additions to Gorelets.com, the ever-evolving website that has grown to become a cavernous digital museum of offbeat wonders.

Consider, for example, "Disco Inferno" and "Driving the Sick Elephant." The first is an animated poem in which words cavort over the landscape of Pieter Brueghel's "Triumph des Todes" (1590), gyrating to a jolting remix of the song "Disco Inferno" by The Trammps. The second is a full-throttle flash fiction reading set to a driving instrumental composition. And although Arnzen reports that he does not put much stock in hit-count reports, it is nonetheless worth noting that Gorelets.com received nearly a half million hits in 2005, an impressive figure in an age when a book of literary fiction is considered a major success when it sells between 30,000 and 50,000 copies (Hoover) and the "average [genre] paperback sells, traditionally, about 15,000 copies" (Flint). By comparison, Arnzen's top-selling novel, the Stoker-winning *Grave Markings*, sold about 30,000 copies in the US (Arnzen, "Re: Book Sales"). Unwilling to settle for such respectable print numbers, Arnzen has, by changing the form and delivery of his literature and seeking readers in the world beyond the realm of books, garnered a wider audience for his poems and stories than he has ever achieved via traditional mass-market venues. The lesson is clear. Contemporary writers would do well to consider Arnzen's success.

Returning for a moment to the models of Faustus and Mephistopheles, one finds that the comparison is not perfect. Arnzen's goal may indeed be to deliver his audience into darkness, but Mephistopheles was a dour entertainer who tricked Faustus into going along on a journey that he ultimately resisted. Arnzen's audience, on the other hand, seems to be enjoying the ride, and Arnzen is anything but dour.

One need only listen to his reading of "Driving the Sick Elephant," complete with the author's own driving rock score (now available on the CD entitled "Audiovile"), to realize how much fun Arnzen is having with his dark mercurial wonders. There is a point, 118 seconds into the reading, where, seeming to suppress a laugh, he says, "And you're getting into it!" Indeed, we are. For a moment, at least, enthralled in his delivery, a few of us may even be willing to burn our books and ride with him on his shape-changing journey, out of the past, through the ether, and into the future.

*

Horror author Lawrence C. Connolly teaches English at Sewickley Prep Academy near Pittsburgh, PA, and is the author of the "Veins" novel series (Fantasist Enterprises). Visit him online at http://lawrencecconnolly.com/

This essay was originally presented at the International Conference for the Fantastic in the Arts 27. "New Directions in Horror" Panel. March 16, 2006 Fort Lauderdale, Florida USA. Subsequently published in DISSECTIONS: The Journal of Contemporary Horror *(Oct 2006) http://www.simegen.com/writers/dissections/*

Works Cited

Arnzen, Michael A. *100 Jolts: Shockingly Short Stories*. Hyattsville, MD: Raw Dog Screaming Press, 2004.

---. *Arnzen's Arbor Vitae*. 1996-9. <http://darkwing.uoregon.edu/~mikea/>.

---. *Chew and Other Ruminations*. Concord, CA: Mastication Publications, 1991.

---. 'Comments.' E-Mail to L. Connolly. 23 Feb 2006.

---. *Grave Markings*. New York: Dell Abyss, 1994.

---. "Introduction." In *Gorelets: Unpleasant Poems*. Fairwood Press: Auburn, WA, 2003. 8-9.

---. "New Media Horror: Six Lessons from an E-Poet." *HWA Newsletter* March/April 2002.

---. "Personal Interview." 2 Feb 2006.

---. "Re: Book Sales." E-mail to L. Connolly. 20 Feb 2006.

---. "Re: Questions Following February 2 Interview." E-Mail to L. Connolly. Feb. 7, 2006.

---. The 'Sickolodeon'. Gorelets. 2006. 5 Feb 2006. <http://www.gorelets.com>.

---. "Unpleasant Poetry: A Retrospective Look." Gorelets. 2006. 4 Feb 2006. <http://www.gorelets.com/gorelets/retro/retro.htm>.

Berners-Lee, Tim. "Short Summary of the World Wide Web Project." 6 Aug 1991. 16 Feb 2006.<http://groups.google.com/group/alt.hypertext/msg/395f282a67a1916c>.

"BitPass Appoints Preston Roper Vice President of Marketing." BitPass. 30 Jan 2006. 5 Feb 2006. <http://prnewswire.com/cgi-bin/stories.pl?ACCT =104&STORY=/www/story/01-30-2006/ 0004269901&EDATE=>.

Clarke, Arthur C. "Quarantine." Isaac Asimov's Science Fiction Magazine (Spring 1977): 49-50.

Flint, Eric. "Increasing sales by offering free eBooks." Planet Ebook. 8 May 2002. 22 Feb 2006. <http://www.planetebook.com/mainpage.asp?webpageid=362>.

Fort, Charles Hoy. "Part One, Chapter Four. Lo! New York: Claude Kendall, 1931." The Fortean Web Site of Mr. X. 1998. 18 Feb 2006. <http://www. resologist.net/lo104.htm>.

Hillesund, Terje. "Will E-books Change the World?" First Monday: Peer-Reviewed Journal of the Internet. October 2001. 16 Feb 2006. <http://www.firstmonday.dk/issues/issue6_10/hillesund/>.

Hoover, Bob. "Overall, we'll miss Oprah's Book Club." Pittsburgh Post-Gazette 14 April 2002. 22 Feb 2006. <http://www.postgazette.com/books/20020414hoover0414fnp2.asp>.

"Horror Author Launches free GORELETS for the PDA!" Geeknews. 8 Aug 2001. 4 Feb 2006. <http://www.geek.com/news/geeknews/2001aug/bpd20010808007182.htm>.

Mayfield, Kendra. "What if E-Books Cost Less?" Wired News. 8 Feb 2001. 17 Feb 2006. <http://www.wired.com/news/culture/0,1284,41633,00.html>.

Reinhardt, Andy. "Momenta Points to the Future." Byte November 1991. 18 Feb 2006. <http://www.byte.com/art/9611/sec4/art1.htm>.

Rose, M.J. Lip Service. New York: Pocket Books, 2001.

Shumate, Peggy Jo, ed. Cemetery Poets: Grave Offerings. Markham, Ontario: Double Dragon Publishing, 2003.

"Who Are We." AmazingMail. 2006. 19 Feb 2006. <http://www.amazingmail.com/about.php?grid=3f0772e10c15af3d>.

Meat Shots, Gorelets, Severed Hands and the Uncanny in Your Inbox: Michael Arnzen's New Directions in Horror
by David Sandner

Frankly, I don't think Michael Arnzen exists.

He's just an excess, just the hack job, cutting across unseen wires into your home. Just a harbinger of the inevitable that we refuse until we, ourselves, are refused and become moot. He's not real; he's an effect. Or, anyway, Arnzen's experiments in form and medium are, I argue, but a necessary response to a problem in the horror genre.

The problem is that it's dead.

All genres experience boom-and-bust cycles. Often a rising wave seems marked by one writer's phenomenal success and a wake of endless imitators and innovators—for horror it was Stephen King in the 1980s. But no genre experienced a bust as hard as horror in the mid-1990s. Horror sections have vanished from bookstores. Horror today can hardly be marketed as horror, except in the smaller presses. In a recent post to his Stoker award-winning Goreletter, Arnzen reviews an anthology that "doesn't call itself a horror anthology," though "if it were published in 1989, it certainly would [have] broadcast its status as one." Instead, the anthology's introduction claims: "Come with us and explore strange new worlds through stories that investigate the darkest of fantasies: a New Weird bathed in classic Gothic eeriness and touched by metaphors of human darkness." Arnzen writes: "one can't help but notice how unsettled it all is about the terminology. Just look at all the synonyms…: strange, dark fantasy, New Weird, Gothic, eerie, dark. There's almost an [overt] attempt to disavow the word 'horror' in all this. But no matter how you slice it, it's scary" ("The Outsider Looking In").

What's scary for Arnzen here? Both, I think, the anthology, reviewed positively, and the disavowal of horror that keeps the editors circling the term like sharks just waiting for it to stop kicking before they feast. Ironically, Arnzen writes about the anthology because it "redraws the boundaries of the horror genre in a very successful way," though not as horror. However, the refusal of horror is, in some ways (though not in other ways that can adversely affect the actual bank accounts of working writers), beside the point. As Arnzen notes elsewhere in his post, horror as a term is a "marketing label," not the same thing as the "genre, *per se*." While horror as a marketing category is moribund in mainstream publishing, the type of fiction it describes, a fiction of fear, bides its time under the bed, sharpening its claws. Or has already emerged under another name. It will not, anyway, long remain nameless. Nor worry long over what name you choose to call it. It will eat you all the same.

As H.P. Lovecraft opens his canonical essay on supernatural horror: "The oldest and strongest emotion of mankind is fear, and the oldest and strongest kind of fear is fear of the unknown. These facts few psychologists will dispute, and their admitted truth must establish for all time the genuineness and dignity of the weirdly horrible tale as a literary form" (102). Here, Lovecraft seeks pride of place for a particular kind of horror story for which he would prove to be the foremost practitioner—and any argument that is self-serving should give us pause. Also, we can certainly note how unsettled the terminology is for Lovecraft as for our unnamed anthology's editors; I, for one, would not recommend calling one's stories "weirdly horrible" as a generic label. But the point, I think, is made, and well taken. If not the oldest emotion, fear is foundational to our existence for all kinds of reasons, many having to do, finally, with our mortality. We need to write about that. Horror literature is the result, no matter how, as Arnzen put it, "you slice it[.]"

The genre of the undead will stick its hand out of the earth eventually. But where? And what will it look like? What monstrous thing, rich and strange, will it be after lying fallow so long? What black flower will bloom from that blood-red earth? The great collapse of the field opens up opportunities to re-imagine the genre, and so, after the wailing and sackcloth, can bring a sense of excitement (that is, until your house payment comes due).

One reason horror busted so hard is that its demise came at a time of upheaval in the process of making and selling books. Technology is moving and reshaping the landscape of entertainment; literature in general is seeking its most profitable future after the rise of video gaming and other forms of immersive electronic entertainment; all literary genres have been affected negatively; and horror found its particular problems of oversaturation of the market compounded. E-literature lurks as a currently unprofitable medium but with potential. But how we read e-literature is going to be different than how we read print. Not necessarily in the radical way foretold by some e-ophile prophets before the computer industry suffered its own bust, but profoundly different nonetheless. We will read differently. We will sell and buy words differently. The experiment to discover how is already under way.

Arnzen's experiments sending poetry—what he has called "Gorelets"—to Palm Pilot in-boxes or with writing short-short "flash" fiction or "jolts" that can appear in online webzines are representative. In his Introduction to his print collection of e-poetry, collectively titled *Gorelets*, Arnzen writes: "...part of my goal [is] to get more readers in the digital age to take notice of poetry. When I began this project I realized that e-books (texts intended to be read on PDAs) were everywhere, but none of them were poetry. And poetry just seemed to 'fit' the screen better than long, eternally scrolling documents written for print rather than pixels" (9). In an online interview reprinted in the appendix of his Stoker-award-nominated collection *100 Jolts*, Arnzen notes: because readers "aren't patient enough (or even visually equipped) to read long pieces on screen...flash fiction is ideal for the electronic marketplace" ("On Writing Flash Fiction" 148-9). Describing his own conversion narrative to writing flash, Arnzen explains: "I finally came to realize that e-publishing is one market opportunity among many that are offered to writers, and with the rising affordability of handheld computers (e.g. e-book readers) and broadband internet, I saw the light" (148). Arnzen's experiments in flash and gorelets mark an attempt to reconfigure, or just figure out, the horror market and deliver an affordable fiction; no small matter. But his experiments cut deeper than that.

The medium shapes the art, after all, at least as much, if not far more than, any ideal dictate of "aesthetics" alone; money, what can be produced and distributed as well as what readers want, decides the form of art that will be marketed most successfully. Flash and gorelets mark a change in form. As Arnzen notes, because print magazines pay by the word, writers have an economic incentive for writing longer works. But, he writes, "the 'new economy' on the internet" [rewards] "those who can write tightly. People who read on-screen don't want to scroll a lot, so longer stories just don't work well online. The form is influencing the market and the genre as a whole" ("On Writing Flash Fiction" 149). Jolts and gorelets are designed to "fit" with current technological media, instead of being translated into them. Arnzen's flash fiction and e-poetry, in other words, are demonstrating the effect of technology on horror writing. And as it affects how we work, and how we buy, and how we read, won't it affect what we fear?

Horror is dead. Long live horror.

Paradoxically, while the future expands before us, the horror field, as represented by the Horror Writer's Association (HWA), contracts. Arnzen's e-newsletter, "The Goreletter," won the 2004 Stoker Award for Best Alternative Form. In his acceptance speech, Arnzen ended with a plea: "This category may very well be odd, but it's also important. We are living in an era of alternative forms, and I would like to think that this category allows us to not only recognize that fact, but also remain actively engaged in our era. Ultimately, horror, too, is an alternative form in the literary marketplace." Soon after, the HWA voted to eliminate the alternative form category. The Goreletter was also a finalist for the last award granted in 2005. As those outside the field have trouble knowing what horror is because they can't find anything called horror widely available in mainstream bookstores, and those inside the genre turn away from experiments that aim to discover what fiction, what poetry—what words in what order—what jolt, what flash, what gorelet, what odd bit of word play—scares us now, pressure builds, I think, to turn to Arnzen's experiments, to the words themselves, whether in ink or flickering light, and try to say what we can say about how they mean and what they have to tell us about new directions in horror literature.

An emphasis on structure is characteristic, on a number of levels, including of course as a practical response to the shape allowed by the e-mediums involved—but also in the sense of finding what kind of horror belongs in such mediums—what themes, what narratives work granted certain parameters. In an interview, "On Writing Flash Fiction," Arnzen comments that he doesn't want to write "long stories masquerading as short ones, but fiction that exploits the limitations of space" (148). For such brief works, extreme limitations of space must not be a limitation at all, but an unrealized advantage to be exploited. But how? Here's an example: in Arnzen's poetry collection parody of *Martha Stewart Living* titled *Michael Arnzen's Dying*, the poems are designed to read like helpful tips, if you happened to be a psychopath. Here's the "handy" advice in tip number 6:

> Don't sweat the small stuff.
> And it's all small stuff:
> eardrums, thumbnails, kidneys,
> elbow nuggets, toe knuckles, eyeballs.
> Let them go.

The shortness of the poetry matches the brevity of the actual tips one might encounter in a home-maker's magazine, perhaps running along the side in its own column, marked out by a bold background color, or organized at the end of a longer article so one needn't actually read the article. The home-maker or psychopath on the go in our modern rush-rush society doesn't have time to read a whole essay of advice, so the well laid-out "tip" with brief generic advice will have to suffice. The implicit idea is: one already knows what the article would say in its details anyway—in other words, one doesn't read it for new advice, but to reinforce one's identity in the brief time allowed in the day to do such things. The brevity is possible because the "tip" is only a reminder of who one already is—of something familiar. Yes, the well-placed tip says, I am a frugal, thoughtful, well-organized homemaker/psychopath—I am the best me I can be.

The blandness of the self-help advice here is typical, and even necessary, then, to the form: "Don't sweat the small stuff./ And it's all small stuff:/... Let them go." The reader is assumed to be obsessive—whether, as in the parodied genre of *Living*, trying to live up to the inhuman home-making standards modeled by Stewart herself, or in the darker way a serial killer may "ritually" mark or clean or keep trophies from a body in oddly particular ways. The advice is so nondescript that it does not ask one to deal with root causes of one's unease—why one is cleaning the same clean countertop for the twentieth time, say, or, you know, murdering someone for no discernible reason. Instead, one is asked to simply identify and alleviate the symptom. One doesn't want to cure one's self—one is only trying to become a better version of what one already is. And what one is is run by the obsession; like a machine, one does what one is told. But one doesn't want to know that—to know that one is not a rugged individualist, not an American in God-given pursuit of personal happiness, not a bold seeker of bliss, but programmed, pre-packaged, a commodity of our shared culture, someone summed up by a series of 'tips' in a magazine.

In Arnzen's poem, the blandness of the bracketing advice is countered by the surprising specificity of the list in the middle of what one should let go: "eardrums, thumbnails, kidneys,/ elbow nuggets, toe knuckles, eyeballs." I'm not sure I know what an elbow nugget is—but I am uncomfortable that someone has thought long enough about it to need the word to identify a certain kind of thing discovered more than once in different elbows. The words are all multisyllabic, requiring me to read them out, to notice them, to "chew" on the long doubled vowels or diphthongs—"ea," "ai", "ey", "oe", "eye"—or even the "e" to start "elbow." One gnaws on the off-beat internal rhyme of "eardrums, thumbnails" that begins the list and then crunches the hard-sounding "kidn", "gget", "toe", "ucles." Numerous alliterations from the "n" in "kidneys," "nuggets" and "knuckles", to the "t" in "nuggets" and "toe" to the "l" in "knuckles" and "eyeballs", serve as connective matter from word to word, but not through the whole line, slowing down one's reading as if one cut through gristle. Arnzen's specific list subverts the blandness of the advice that precedes and follows it, the advice that is itself an attempt to disavow the horror of the list and mediate it; but the mediation is itself an awful thing: one is horrified that someone would attempt to be so calm, so clean and neat, so everyday, in the aftermath of a brutal murder. Then, of course, one may realize that murders, cruel and savage, do occur every day—they are normal. They are bland. Reading a poem, now *that's* abnormal.

The poem is uncanny in its bland inability to cover the horror of our physical bodies—their decay and death—like a corpse inexpertly hid under the floorboards, its heart refusing to stop beating in one's ears. What one doesn't want to think about, murder, and the simple fact of death become familiar again; and our familiar "living" selves, sweeping up our homes, doing our dishes, become nothing but murderers cleaning those tough spots on our bloodied hands or just corpses cleaning their graves—we are already dead, already helpless before death, and before our love of death that leads us to kill one another every day. This theme, the uncanny return of the body in all its messy "bodiness" against the ineffective mediation of words, of culture, of technology, of all idealizations that try to move us toward abstraction and away from our smelly, gurgling selves, is characteristic of Arnzen's work. Not new in horror, of course, it may nonetheless be the kind of horror those in the grip of the promise of new technology and its seeming power and mastery over the world needs to hear.

The brevity has the purpose of making the reader realize the story for themselves, to imagine; the plot is not overlooked in flash fiction, but rather implied. An attention to plot is a hallmark of genre fiction; the shape of the plot reveals which genre one is reading; flash fiction is so short that one must supply the story by already knowing it, by being familiar with a genre and its workings. Flash and gorelets are not simply brief. Instead, the short work hints at more—reading these hints requires the active participation of readers who already know the full story, who will guess at it and work it up themselves. These short works, in short, are fragments broken from something larger—they have an implied structure, even if much of it is out of sight. Consider this odd gorelet, "Fuzzy Bunnies":

> the eyes roll back
> and accusingly glare
> when my feet slide forward
> and hot rabbit innards
> squirt between my toes
>
> only then do I see
> why these furry white skins
> are called slippers.

Trying to figure out the context here for us to "slip" our reading experience inside is part of what is disconcerting here. Crucial to any reading is the pun at the end—the slippers, so-called because we "slip" them on our feet easily, without time-consuming laces or buckles, becomes instead a foot "slipping" into wet, apparently at least still semi-living actual bunnies. The dead eyes accuse us of forgetting what should have been obvious—the opening here is a wound. The pun marks the important move toward "closure" that is necessary to the form. If the gorelet or flash fiction is to have a larger structure, it must not present only unconnected detail, but seek an ending, a hit, a moment of *frisson*. In horror, the payoff often requires violence.

If fantasy might have something called a sense of wonder which throws one outward to imagine something else, something new, what we have here might be horror's sense of dismembering, both a tearing apart and a remembering of what we long to forget. The bunny's accusing stare makes one see it is staring at us, and has been all along. The gorelet or flash fiction often seeks its ending in the violent "meat shot," the sudden realization of the body through words that of course can never deliver an actual body. The subversive quality of horror is called into play to jolt us out of the trance of reading to realize our breathing, rotting selves, the forgotten reader implied by any story, no longer allowed to be only something packed in behind the eyeballs, no longer just an ideal self, carried in a meat container that unfortunately limits us—but the return to the fact that we are simply the eyeball, the meat container itself. A realization long and strenuously denied comes upon us suddenly, a "meat shot" indeed.

The poem is accompanied by the familiar picture of one fuzzy bunny slipper against a background of the deepest black. In a newspaper interview, Arnzen recounts that his grandmother had asked him to write about fuzzy bunnies—she should have known better, I think (Williams 4). The poem is, dear grandma, about fuzzy bunnies—but moves to the wet, squishy innards hidden beneath the soft fur that only becomes visible when the poor thing is badly wounded or cut open and dead. Uncanny—homely and horrific— the glass eyes mock our eyes and suggest our glassy dead stares to come; the sewed on smiles become all the more faked in a time of fear, when the human reaction should be something quite different, we like to think, but will become the sameness of the skullhead's grimace for us all.

Lastly, consider the flash fiction from *100 Jolts*, "Amputating the Phantom," beginning with the straightforward scene-setter: "I chop off his arms." The decapitating narrator is mesmerized by the stare of his victim and feels "his phantom hands, beating me...." The story ends with the narrator batting the phantom limbs away "before I move to chop again at the neck, wondering if this will ever stop, wondering if I have a phantom self who is cowering in pain and dying away even as I swing the blade." The self-reflexivity is a hint of course. Who is really staring at the narrator? We are—the reader. The character cuts out at us. But we control him with our stares, our eyes flicking from side to side. We make him perform his role, and if we have questions, or just enjoyed it enough, we shoot our look upward to the top of the page (for it is but one page) and start over, making the narrator perform his pain again. The answer is yes, we do have a phantom self who is dying away even as we read—we have a body we have set aside in our eagerness for the story. Reading here is like shaking hands to find only the severed hand in your grasp. The severed hand is something that was a part of us, so crucial to our identity—think of your fingerprint—but a part that is chopped off, separated from us, and we are still we, aren't we?—and it is now it. The severed hand acting on its own impulses after its separation is the uncanny reminder of our fear, maybe even, I should say, our knowledge, that this is already so. For the hand, severed or not, you see, has its own agency. We just don't want to admit it. It is us. It is under our control. Until it isn't. Whether through spasms. Or you sleep on it until it falls asleep, becoming for a time a thing attached to you that you must flop and drag about. Or you chop it off.

The horror fragments, jolts, sudden fictions, gorelets offered by Arnzen have their own agency as well. We read them, we take them for ours, are even asked to complete the full arc of the narrative moment shown to us, but then they cut us with phantom knives held in severed hands. Arnzen's "minimalist" jolts of prose/poetry are designed to easily re-conform to the restrictions of, and thus to insinuate itself into, our systems of new technology. Originally available in numerous forms from traditional print to underground webzines to online at his Stoker-winning website to email sent at random times to the in-boxes of subscribers' Palm Pilots, Arnzen's innovations have implications at once for the future evolution of horror as a genre seeking to survive cyclical implosions of popularity in traditional print markets and as a harbinger of the kind of horror conjured up by our technophilic age. Arnzen's horror cuts at the body with short, sharp sentences, fragments of narrative, his words dismembering, reconfiguring, returning us to our forgotten flesh but rendering it strange to us with a sudden violence, a spurt of text, a cracked narrative, a shock at the ending "meat shot," the fatal blow all the more terrible because undercut by a fatalistic and devious humor. We prefer to not think too closely about our bodies, their aging and dying, their fragile systems of organs and bones strung together with muscle; we prefer to think of our essence as located "somewhere else," somewhere abstracted, more permanent. We use machines to expand our reach, to extend ourselves through the vast electronic web of information that connects us and confirms us. Arnzen's short horror, with its compactness of effect, turns our insular systems of control, internal and external, psychological and technological, against us for, if we are careful readers, our intense amusement at the frailty of our own illusions and a shocked satisfaction of desires we might wish we never had.

So, don't look now: you have mail.

*

Dr. David Sandner teaches English Literature at California State University at Fullerton when he's not otherwise writing funky sci-fi or criticism of the literary fantastic. His books include *The Fantastic Sublime and Critical Discourses of the Fantastic, 1712-1831*. *This essay was originally presented at the International Conference for the Fantastic in the Arts 27. "New Directions in Horror" Panel. March 16, 2006 Fort Lauderdale, Florida USA. Subsequently published in* DISSECTIONS: The Journal of Contemporary Horror *(Oct 2006): http://www.simegen.com/writers/dissections/*

Works Cited

Arnzen, Michael A. "Acceptance Speech for Bram Stoker Award 2004 (Alternative Forms)" Delivered 5 June 2004, Park Central Hotel, New York. Archived online. <www.gorelets.com>

---. "Amputating the Phantom." In *100 Jolts: Shockingly Short Stories*. Hyattsville, MD: Raw Dog Screaming Press, 2004. 92.

---. "Fuzzy Bunnies." In *Gorelets: Unpleasant Poems*. Auburn, WA: Fairwood Press, 2003. 23.

---. "Introduction." In *Gorelets: Unpleasant Poems*. Auburn, WA: Fairwood Press, 2003. 8-9.

---. *Michael Arnzen's Dying*. San Francisco, CA: Tachyon Publications, 2003.

---. "On Writing Flash Fiction." In *100 Jolts: Shockingly Short Stories*. Hyattsville, MD: Raw Dog Screaming Press, 2004. 148-53.

---. "The Outsider Looking In." *The Goreletter* 3.05 (27 Nov 2005).Archived online. <www.gorelets.com>

Lovecraft, H.P. "Introduction to Supernatural Horror in Literature (1927)." In *Fantastic Literature: A Critical Reader*. Ed. David Sandner. Westport, CT: Praeger, 2004. 102-5.

Williams, Drew. "Seton Hill Prof Scares Up Some Laughs: An Interview with Michael Arnzen." *Laurel Mountain Post* (Fall 2005): 4-5.

Domestic Dissection:
Michael Arnzen's Domestic Horror

by Gina Wisker

Mike Arnzen's minimalist horror fiction and poetry cuts straight through the artifice of domestic and romantic relationships, revealing a disturbing core of dis-ease, decapitation, dismemberment, dismay. His use of horror, "the genre of the undead" (*100 Jolts*, 11) is shockingly contemporary, yet follows in the tradition of others who take the everyday, the domestic, and disturb our complacencies, notably Edgar Allen Poe, H.P Lovecraft, and Stephen King. Identifying horror's differences from crime fictions, he notes:

> Horror's mysteries are usually universally repressed truths, whereas suspense is a piano chord that can only be played so long. Horror bangs on the same piano as suspense, but it produces more chaotic chords. Cacophony, sometimes. Horror pounds the keys of the literary piano in staccato rhythm. Horror resides in the chirp of the *Psycho* soundtrack. The arc of Mother's knife. And the pulse-racing dribble and twist of the camera down the drain afterwards. (*100 Jolts*, 10)

This homes in on the discomfort of domestic horror, which explores those repressed truths, the disorientation when what has been taken for granted as dependable—home, hearth, family, children, partner, parents, the conventional safety of a suburban everyday—are revealed as only constructions held in place tenuously by our beliefs, and just as likely to be displaced and undercut as are predictions of the weather.

Arnzen's work features fast food outlets, babies as playthings, a zombie anniversary meal celebrating six millennia, the preservation of the body of a dead beloved wife. All of these are both topical and, differently contextualised, traumas and concerns of the human condition. The tone of the stories is laced with the threateningly macabre, the deadly interlinking of gender and power politics, poison and bodily rupture reminiscent of the revenge tragedians of the Renaissance: Webster, Tourneur, Shakespeare, and of the Gothic streak in Romantic and Victorian poetry. So we are reminded of Keats' "Isabella and the Pot of Basil," her lover's head growing herbs after her brothers' brutal rejection, when in Arnzen's "Gardener" the wife clips the husband's spinal cord, prunes the skull, and grows tomatoes in his head. "I hated every single word he spoke," she begins and clips his spinal cord, turns him into a vegetable then neglects him, and finally pruning his skull: "then I turned him upside down and grew tomatoes in his potted head" (*100 Jolts*). While the Keats tale emphasizes the power of the brothers to prevent romance and love, this minimalist fiction by Mike Arnzen focuses on the irritations of long term domesticity, in which revenge of a particular horticultural kind both emphasizes the domestic (tomatoes growing from his skull) and undermines any sense of nurturance in relationships. The gardening motif returns, with the garden box burial of a husband who won't share childcare in "Taking Care of Baby" (*100 Jolts*). The irritated husband demands that the wife deal with the baby when it screams at night. It is not his responsibility, in his view. In the second stanza, she emphasizes his uselessness as a support of her hard work, getting revenge out of her resentment: "He screams from the box beneath my garden bed, pounding: 'Babe, will you please open this thing up?'" This companion piece to his insistence that she "shut that thing up" when baby cried a little earlier, gives her back the power, turns the tables. The husband fulfills the promise of his vegetative state.

Domestic horror is particularly threatening to our tenuously held notions of the *status quo* because it attacks us where we need to feel most secure, in the supermarket with its muzak as much in the lounge, garden, playpen. Domestic horror has a sound pedigree. It picks on an innate need for safety, the complacent assumption that social obedience and common sense reward us. However, as Stephen King points out:

>...the good horror tale will dance its way to the center of
>your life and find the secret door to the room you believed
>no one but you knew of. (King 149)

Using and disturbing the comfortable location of the home, King indicates both the horror of place and the horror of self. The room at the center of our life is our own identity, our sanity, our sense of stability of self. But in domestic horror the revelation is that those around us and the places in which we live no longer reflect and resonate with safety and certainty but instead leak disturbance and dismay. Domestic spaces such as rooms, homes, beds, are choice locations for horror primarily because of the safety, security and familiarity they promise. Disturbing these certainties fundamentally undercuts identity and ontological security. Jung, in aligning the self with the house, home, or living space, opened up a gap for disturbance and terror, for insecurity and questioning. In horror, there are direct connections between insecurity, stability, identity and the house or home. Horror takes the Gothic fascination with locations straight into our most intimate and personal spaces. Virginia Andrews' terrifying *Flowers in the Attic* (1979) is a disturbing example of this—as it involves incarceration, child abuse and neglect at the heart of the family relationships and domestic spaces—exactly where you would hope to find nurturance. Following the death of their father, the Dollenganger children, twins and a brother and sister, are incarcerated by their untrustworthy mother in an attic in their grandmother's house. The bullying, puritanical grandfather is to be feared and avoided, even the mother is terrified of him and he must never know of the existence of the children. Inheritance and heritage are dangerous, diseased, threatened, rather than celebrated in this narrative situation. The spiteful, violent grandmother clearly hates the idea of children and particularly hates a union of uncle and niece (their parents), which she finds blasphemous. The walls of the children's attic are covered with scenes from hell. They cannot escape until it is almost too late for all four of them, and gradually wither away. Neglect instead of nurturance, brutality, the starving of affection and condemnation of identity instead of love and care are the experience of these children's lives.

Mike Arnzen's fictional children similarly experience neglect and sometimes plain destruction. So in "Stress Toy" a child is misinterpreted as entertainment, the location for the emotional dysfunctions of a modern couple. Hubby and Wifey contemplate the new stress toy which has been delivered to help minimize anxieties at work. It is ugly, boxed and new, a gift, an object on which to offload destructive energies so that the modern self can survive intact. Each examine it with disgust. Because of its named function, "stress toy," there is license here to treat the toy as brutally as the husband wishes, in order to relieve his stress. They are legitimated in this by the directions on the box. At his comment: "A squeeze toy? You mean I just throttle it and that relieves stress?" (*100 Jolts*, 52) the toy rolls its eyes up at the couple, belying its existence as mere object, disturbing the reader, indicating that its status and treatment are a construction, an excuse for their cruelty. Their smiling down at the creature inside the box reveals their collusion in their acts of neglect and violence. To the reader the awful truth is that the creature is actually alive. Children, for this is clearly a child, are revealed stress relievers, squeeze toys, something to confirm the sense of control and relief for their parents. This creature/object can legitimately be brutalized because of its confused status as a toy but the language reveals its human characteristics and the deliberate collusion of the couple as an ignoring of such characteristics:

> she squeezes, [and] the executive toy whimpers before its chest puffs out and its eyes bulge all googly from the squeezing. Its arms and legs swat and swim in the air. Wifey waits until the toy's head turns to purple so she can see the veins pattern and throb on the scalp. "See?"' (52)

Demon and deadly children are as common as their deadly parents. In the poem "The Suckling" (*Gorelets* 57), in a travesty of the birth experience, a newborn creature is born into a crypt, sucks off its own umbilical cord as its undead mother comforts and feeds it, so:

> His mother lines his mouth
> With a handful of leeches
> And cradles the undead child
> In her pale lithe arms to feed.

Families are threatening, deadly. Domestic spaces and the homely locations of mall, café, suburbs, family house, are all deceptive, liable to erupt, implode, suck you into some terrible experience, punish you for some previous ill deed. Horror frequently exposes and explodes familiar locations as confined when they would be nurturing and safe, threatening where we would have them as confirmatory of security, of being and self—exposing the family, home, attic, cellar, kitchen, bedroom, toilet, garden and neighborhood as danger zones. Horror also undermines our sense of reality by transforming what is considered "real" through exposing what is feared and hidden. In doing so, spatial descriptors become important, deploying what Freud defines as "paraxis." Rosemary Jackson explores those Gothic horror spaces as indicators of alternative truths revealed *in situ*, on location, exposing this notion of an underside or alternative space as beyond, beneath, or above the recognizably ordinary, thus figuring the home, office, bedroom, fast food outlet, playpen, garden, and the suburbs themselves as actually much less secure and safe than we need them to be:

> Fantasy lies alongside the axis of the real, and many of
> the prepositional constructions which are used to introduce
> a fantastic realm emphasize its interstitial placing, "On
> the edge", "through", "beyond", "between", "at the back
> of", "underneath" or adjectives such as "topsy-turvy",
> "reversed", "inverted." (Jackson 64)

Domestic horror frequently uses adjectives suggesting invasion/explosion/ disturbance of those spaces, a cracking of the secure fabric to reveal gaps, fissures, and leakages, indicating contradictions and threats to what then appears a kind of culpably naïve investment in domestic and personal security. Such are the contemporary threats to Middle America and other Western urban and suburban locations, the neighborhoods of comfortable families, 2.4 children, and their baby-sitters. In horror, such locations harbor axe murderers, psychotics (*Halloween*, *A Nightmare on Elm Street*), terrible secrets, villages of alien children, and plants that pick up their roots, chase, and eat people (John Wyndham's *The Midwich Cuckoos*, *The Day of the Triffids*), crazed pets (*Cujo*), demonic domestic appliances or family cars (*From a Buick 8*, *Christine*), household walls that reach out grab and haul in the crazed lone individual (Polanski's *Repulsion*). For Stephen King, among others, what is fascinatingly played out is the unsettling character of Middle America, its lurking fears, and the disturbance of its complicity in all that would undermine its façade of order. For British writers John Wyndham, Dennis Wheatley, and Angela Carter, parents are likely to sell daughters' souls to the devil (Wheatley, *To the Devil a Daughter*), homes are likely to need the protection of a magic circle (Wheatley, *The Devil Rides Out*), uncles locate performative spaces in their cellars and try to turn nieces into puppets and rape victims (Angela Carter, *The Magic Toyshop*).

Alfred Hitchcock urges us to "put back horror where it belongs, in the family" (exhibition, Sydney museum of art, 1998). Entrapment, engulfment, monstrous parents and equally monstrous children, skeletons in closets and chopped messes on the kitchen table are all features of domestic horror that focus on the oppressive, the threatening, the perverse, and the sickening flip side of "domestic bliss."

Edgar Allan Poe, Angela Carter, Joyce Carol Oates, Stephen King, Melanie Tem, Virginia Andrews, among a range of horror writers, concentrate on domestic horror, as do a range of films depicting family horrors in enclosed spaces (e.g., *The Shining*, *The Exorcist*, *The Omen*, *Rosemary's Baby*, and *The Village of the Damned*), set in apartment blocks, hotels, homes, pleasant country villages, and which variously focus on mad monster fathers, changeling children—usually the devil's own offspring (or aliens) and invasion of the domestic home. Domestic horror exposes the contradictions and potential/real unpleasantness of domestic settings and relationships, of nuclear and extended families, of romance, marriage and parenting. It focuses in particular on the unsafe neighborhood, the ostensibly loving but actually non-nurturing home as sites for horror. It re-represents parents, partners and children as variously deceptive, destructive, invasive, life-denying.

What is so terrifying about domestic horror? The horror of the disruption of the everyday world? Why might the family home, intimate relationships and parenting be a site for horror when on them depend our sense of safety, continuity, comfort, and familiarity—a reflection of ourselves, of our sense of security, and, through our children a sense of some kind of identity, heredity, immortality? Domestic horror is terrifying and disturbing precisely for those reasons. The qualities and certainties we desire from domestic life, relationships and families, reveal our vulnerabilities as we try to construct safe havens, continuities of self and relationships, and believe that we ward off the dark. The stuff of horror operates through the removal or undercutting of these securities and certainties which keep out the dark. We are all concerned with security, trust, ontological certainty, the immortality children offer us. Beneath that sort of comfort lie the fears of parasitic children, domineering husbands, incarceration in the threatened home, nurturing turned to abuse or neglect. "Domestic bliss" has of course been critiqued by feminism as well as popular fiction, after the feminist recognition that "You start by sinking into his arms and you end up with your arms in his sink." In horror, of course, you might end up with your body parts in his fridge. Mike Arnzen is certainly influenced by such post-feminist revelations, as you might imagine a lecturer who teaches today's students to be. In Arnzen's minimalist fictions and poetry, housework and domestic or suburban locations feature, just as many demonic and collusive wives, partners and husbands, as strangers. In fact, the closer the relative, the more dangerous and destructive they tend to be.

Everyday terrors enter each seemingly safe familiar world. As the protagonist passes the time, his daughter playing among colored plastic balls suddenly retrieves the first of several human skulls. The young daughter retrieving skulls from among the playzone, colored balls in the local fast food chain

("Skull Fragments", *100 Jolts*, 2004) exposes the proximity of death, destruction, hidden horrors in the safety of contemporary life. The bizarre pops up in the everyday:

> Her favorite continent in Playland is the giant pen full of plastic balls which she loves to dive into and hide within, only to leap back out and scare other children whenever they enter the bin. You eat a burger and it's business as usual, until you hear her scream. Authentically. You turn, and for only a moment you think she's found some strange sort of puppet. But you quickly realize: your daughter holds a real human skull in her hands. (Arnzen, *100 Jolts*, 12)

This is the first of such skulls. Genocide, and serial killings are brought into play spaces, safe spaces, revealing both their artifice and the numbing secrets of a world of danger, engulfment, the monstrous, around us everywhere.

Arnzen's texts which form the recently produced short films anthology, *Exquisite Corpse* (2006), reveal the inequalities of childcare sharing, the deadly potential of sado-masochistic sexual games, and the implications of covert desires for total mind, body, soul manipulation and ownership fuelling the fetishistic objectification of representation of the loved one, capturing and preserving the moment, in the picture, in art. The poem, "Artistic License," is particularly revealing. Reminiscent of the powerful Duke's turning his wife into a portrait only he can own in Browning's "My Last Duchess," and Poe's deadly painter who focuses on the portrait rather than the (neglected, soon dead) wife, a post-modernist painter uses as paint the bloodsplatter of the model he shoots point blank, needing to own her "perfect eyes" in his "perfect portrait," plugging, daubing, fixing, her "piercing stare," matched by the way he "pierces her clean through/the skull lodging a slug right between/ the eyes of his perfect portrait."

Where is horror? It is all around us, and in the places we wish were most secure:

It's in black-jacketed books and lurid movie posters. It's in
police reports from murder sites and tearful recollections
from battlefields. It's in our nightmares. It's in our secret
ambitions. (Barker 16)

And in Mike Arnzen's work it is in our beds, our playpens, our homes,
ourselves. A man threatens to microwave the cat, promising his neighbor his
is an oven that is different, remote controlled, and in a smart move, turns the
waves outside, microwaving his loathed neighbor ("Next-door", *100 Jolts*).
A wife lunges at her husband with a pizza cutter, his body stinging from the
garlic and peppers, his remains delivered in cardboard like a take-out pizza.
"It was then [he realizes, that] she liked her men cold and leftover" ("Take
Out," *100 Jolts*). Arnzen's zombie couples in "Night-Married" have no need
to swear eternal love. Theirs will continue as the undead throughout time,
snacking on each other's attire, with a disarmingly gossipy tone undermined
by the disgusting abject details:

> She wed the zombie too young

We are informed, and she is awoken nightly, in a domestic scenario, by his
cold feet.

> Yet his love will never die so long as
> She nurtures him with the cow brains
> She dons for dinner like a wet wig (*Gorelets* 49)

Arnzen reveals romance and representation as violent invasion, ownership,
fetishism of body parts, dismemberment of the whole person, the opposite
of the intimate completion and reassurance of popular belief. His domestic
bliss reveals babies as brutalized playthings, marriage as a gendered war
of power play, deceit, dire revelations, engulfment, an eternity locked in a

deadly embrace. As he dissects the domestic, so he disturbs our equilibrium. The home and family will never seem so comforting again.

*

Gina Wisker is Head of the Centre for Learning and Teaching and Professor of Higher Education and Contemporary Literature at the University of Brighton (UK) where she teaches literature and manages educational development. Gina writes on postcolonial, contemporary and genre fictions. Her latest book is a *Reader's Guide to Margaret Atwood* available from Continuum Books. She is the editor in chief of *Dissections* journal at: http://www.simegen.com/ writers/dissections/

This essay was originally presented at the International Conference for the Fantastic in the Arts 27. "New Directions in Horror" Panel. March 16, 2006 Fort Lauderdale, Florida USA. Subsequently published in DISSECTIONS: The Journal of Contemporary Horror *(Oct 2006): http://www.simegen.com/writers/dissections/*

Works Cited

Andrews, VC. *Flowers in the Attic*. New York: Pocket Books, 1979.

Arnzen, Michael A. *Gorelets: Unpleasant Poems*. Fairwood Press: Auburn, WA, 2003.

---. *100 Jolts: Shockingly Short Stories*. Hyattsville, MD: Raw Dog Screaming Press, 2004.

---. *Exquisite Corpse: An International Collaboration of Dark Cinema*. DVD. Producer Jim Minton. Poeticollage/The Jim Minton Design Group, 2006.

Barker, Clive. *Clive Barker's A-Z of Horror*. Ed. Stephen Jones. New York: HarperCollins, 1997.

Jackson, Rosemary. *Fantasy: The Literature of Subversion*. London: Routledge, 1981.

King, Stephen. *Danse Macabre: The Anatomy of Horror*. London: Futura, 1982.

Michael Arnzen's Gorey Experiments
by Rich Ristow

For some poets, composing haiku or tanka as a text message could be a plausible, creative activity. Many traditional Japanese forms are small and subtle, as more is required of them then just a syllable count. Writing them takes an act of controlled deliberation, not the sort of stream of consciousness that comes with fast typing on a keyboard—one has to choose their words carefully. Texting on a cell phone only facilitates slowing the writer down, not only because you can only use one finger to enter the words, but if one does it the hard way, and doesn't insert ready-made and saved words or type in LOL-LMAO text-speak, one has to hit the same button multiple times just to get the right letter. In a sense, the frustrating constraints make the writer actively rethink his word choice, not to mention the direction of the poem he's writing. Also, one's not going to write a sestina on a cell phone either, because the process would become too maddening, and the resulting poem would be too long for a text message. This is just one example of how the methods of writing can sometimes dictate the output.

Basically, every writer eventually creates their own system, and sometimes, they actively seek new ways to constrain themselves. The late A.R. Ammons, for example, tended to compose longer works on a continuous strip of paper. Joe Wenderoth decided, one day, to sit in a Wendy's and compose prose poems on their comment cards, some of which were ponderous, pornographic, absurd, and outright hilarious. The result of that experiment became his book *Letters to Wendy's*.

Then, there's Michael A. Arnzen's chapbook *Gorelets: Unpleasant Poems*. He chose to constrain himself by writing, initially, on his handheld. He writes in his introduction that:

What distinguishes these texts is the way they were written and
the way they were intended to be read: on a portable handheld
computer…Whenever the urge struck, I composed on a 3" x
3" screen with a stylus. Consequently, no poem here is longer
than eleven lines and each of those lines contains eight words at
best…The medium certainly shaped the message. (*Gorelets*)

So, the result was a bunch of short, lean poems, some more experimental than
others. Of course, Arnzen goes on to note one other limiting factor: they had to
be "horror" poems. Much of *Gorelets* stretches between what is grim and what
is goofy, showcasing, at times, a sly sense of humor. But as for the chapbook
itself, the poems are a variety of different techniques. Sure, the PDA and stylus
helped make these poems relatively short, but that doesn't mean that they're all
necessarily the same. For example, there's this tongue twister:

Sunk

squalid skull
spurts silt snot—
sunken sailor
once sneezed
seeking safer
sand

To point out the obvious, the poem runs together the letter "S." The dash
is working like a cutting moment, one that is often found in haiku and tanka.
   Now that's not the same as:

Compost

eggshells and applesauce
blood pudding pies

peanut butter apricots
chicken bone thighs
pine needles pumpkin seeds
potato skin peels
orange rinds coffee grinds
your last meal

There's no punctuation here, except for the line breaks, and that has the effect of running everything together, so the poem creates a larger image. Stephen Dobyns once suggested that point of free verse is to create a system and then undermine it. It's good to think of that as a sucker punch, which is exactly what Arnzen does here. Everything in the poem is a list, except for the last line, which takes on different meanings. For one, "your last meal" can be in or part of the compost heap, or the compost heap literally is "your last meal." If one actually eats the decomposing bacteria ridden parts of a compost heap, it likely will be "your last meal."

Of course, there are other currents running through *Gorelets: Unpleasant Poems*, like what some might call "poetry of the moment." These, in many respects, are more grounded, albeit in a twisted reality. The point, really, is to paint a scene caught in time, without any prolonged narrative impulse:

the oral surgeon removes his mask

and there is no chin
just half a mouth, over-biting air
as if possessing an upper palate
is all it takes to smile
before he cups my jaw in his hands
and presses it wetly into place
a new mask hanging on his false face
and as numb fades into nothing
all I can scream are vowels

The title is part of the humor here, as it effectively uses the convention where the title is part of the poem itself. The rest of the poem follows the notion of a single idea / image per line, as the poem stretches down the page, locking all together in the last line. This is a usual aspect of Arnzen's poetry. The test of a poet, often, is how far he or she can move beyond the limitations that they set for themselves. In that sense, *Gorelets* doesn't read like a bunch of tiny poems that were quickly trotted off on a PDA. They are tiny experiments as to what a poet can do with a minuscule amount of space, and even with only a tiny amount of space, Arnzen's possibilities are limitless.

*

This essay originally appeared on the Casual Pundit *weblog in 2008: http://casualpundit.wordpress.com/2008/09/28/michael-arnzens-gorey-experiments/*

Bloody Red Wheelbarrows
by Rich Ristow

"The Red Wheelbarrow" is one of the most important poems in American poetry. If one looks at the history of American free verse, two luminaries stand at the forefront of modernism. William Carlos Williams and Ezra Pound did all they could to hasten the decline of metrical poetry as the accepted norm, and their efforts paved the way for the image-based free verse employed by contemporaries like Nikki Giovanni, Charles Simic, Yusef Komunyaakaa, and many, many others…like Michael A. Arnzen. Basically, if one's writing simple free-verse in this day and age, you're under the influence of Williams, even if you've never read him. There's a simple way of proving this. Consider:

The Red Wheelbarrow

So much depends
upon

a red wheel
barrow

glazed with rain
water

besides the white
chickens.

The above is so simplistic, it drives many people batty. Usually, the maddened exclamation is "This is not poetry, goddamn it!" Most complain Williams, his red wheelbarrow, and his white chickens are trivial at best. There's no dramatic, sweeping soul searching that one finds in, say, Shakespeare or John Donne. Still, the above poem is probably one of the most important written in the last hundred years. It is important for its innovation. Pound and Williams were actively looking for alternatives to rhyming syllabic meter. They wanted to dispose of the old metrical system. So they looked to Asia, particularly the poetry of Japan and China, where subtlety and image are driving factors. For example, consider this haiku:

An old pond
a frog jumps in
the sound of water

—Matsuo Basho

As readers, we don't know if the frog is jumping into the "old pond" or into the "sound of water." One can make valid cases either way, but there's no conclusive evidence. The most important thing here is the construction of the haiku itself. Granted, there is some nitpicker who would read the above Basho poem and cluck their tongue at me.

"Rich," they would say, "That's not a haiku. Haiku are poems of 17 syllables, following a 5-7-5 pattern." Such critics would go on to say, that the following is a better haiku poem:

my old grandmother (5)
made spaghetti every day (7)
of her daily life. (5)

Bullshit! (And on so many levels!)

The spaghetti nonsense is not haiku. Traditionally, the 17 syllable requirement is for haiku in Japanese, where words are more polysyllabic. A lot of polysyllabic words cannot fit into a mere 17 syllables. English, on the other hand, uses more monosyllabic words. So, if one is using the 17 syllable guideline, it violates the classic intent. It is easier to be wordy in seventeen English syllables. In Japanese, the nature of language makes wordiness harder. If you're writing haiku in Japanese, you can't stuff a lot into the three lines.

In haiku, contrasting and juxtaposing imagery is always more important. With Basho's poem, you have three images: a pond, a frog, and "the sound of water." the images have to be in that order, because by the time you hit the third line, all of it locks together into one total image. This is the same dynamic often found in Chinese poetry, too. (Although, now, with translators hard at work, we can now see this in classical Korean and Vietnamese poetry, too).

So, let's look at "The Red Wheelbarrow" again:

> So much depends
> upon
>
> a red wheel
> barrow
>
> glazed with rain
> water
>
> besides the white
> chickens

The first two lines are abstractions. Yet, Williams was thinking more about how to break his lines. In essence, these two lines force the reader to read on, because the rest of the poem is pure image, albeit a fractured one. Breaking the lines between "wheel" and "barrow" creates tension, because "a red wheel" is an image by itself, and the next line, "barrow" redefines that image. Still, you read the poem carefully, the same craft employed in haiku is present. This is a series of images that locks together at the end. As for meaning, each line is redefined by what follows it. By the end, we, as readers, see a farm scene, but the first two lines give this a sense of ambiguity, as well as the pretense of a grand statement.

If, as a student of poetry, one were to write this out as prose, the poem becomes wholly uninteresting. Taking out the line breaks gets rid of the organizational tension, and the poem itself becomes a simple declarative sentence. Still, it's from this poem we get the idea of the creative poetic line as the defining organizational tool in free verse. You do not find this organizational dynamic in Shakespeare or Wordsworth. Iambic Pentameter, for example, requires ten syllables. The line ends where it does, but only because the meter says so.

Free verse allows more flexibility. So, it is that Williams' early imagist poetry can be taken as a skeleton key. The mechanics of "The Red Wheelbarrow" can unlock just about any contemporary American free verse-poem.

So, let's see how this stacks up. Here is a poem from Michael A. Arnzen and his email newsletter, "The Goreletter":

The Fall Down the Stairs
of the House of Usher

When I push her down the stairs
she swims in the air for a moment
like we're dancing
and I play a little song in my head
to accompany it
before the erratic thud of her skull
against the steps
breaks my waltzing daydream
with its own offbeat tempo
and I hear another voice sing
as I stumble forward

The first line, "When I push her down the stairs" is one complete action. As a thought, it may not be complete, but as a concept, from the beginning of the line to the end, it is one entire thing. A lot can be inferred from the line. After all, the first person singular "I" is doing the pushing, and "down the stairs" acts as a subtle bit of scenery. Still, the most important thing to remember here is that the action is deliberate. It would be safe to assume that this line is also describing an attempt at murder. This, of course elicits a response:

she swims in the air for a moment

This naturally is a line that's delivering an evocative image. Basically, the woman, the "her" of the poem becomes frantic as she falls, and much of that depends on Arnzen's specific word choice. "She" is "swimming." As an action, that would require either vigorous or leisurely kicking of the legs and waving of the arms. Since, much like the Williams poem, this is building off the line before, we can safely assume that she's wildly flailing. Still, the line break freezes her in the air for a moment. But, then, the poem begins to shift:

like we're dancing

Now this is odd. If we take "swim" at its surface value, the motions are not completely comparable with "dancing." One also needs to keep in mind that the speaker is still at the top of the stairs. Perhaps—and this is a bit of stretch—one thinks of the spastic, flinging motions of jitterbugging or the throws involved in paired figure skating? Still, this line is one unit, one idea, and one motion cue. "We" is also an important word here. A relationship, or a partnership, is inferred by a pronoun like "we." Still, however awkward, the line works as a unit, and the reader sees, for a split second, dancing. While it's a stark contrast with the line preceding it, it flows nicely into:

and I play a little song in my head / to accompany it

These two lines build on the crazy other-reality in the murderer's head. Basically, he's watching her fall, and he's imagining that it's all a song and dance. If one is thinking of the whole WCW concept of line organization, it plays out with another complete action, followed by an idea that redefines that action. "To accompany it" also links the song with the dancing and the falling down the stairs. If the song and the dance is an illusion or imagined, hard reality intercedes quickly:

before the erratic thud of her skull

This is a sonic detail, giving us the definite sound of her head hitting something. More detail ensues:

against the steps

This line redefines the preceding line. Much like in "The Red Wheelbarrow," this is a moment like where Williams is cutting "barrow" off of "red wheel," or towards the end, where he's putting a pause between "white" and "chickens." "Against the steps" redefines "...the erratic thud of her skull" from sound into something that's sound and image. "The steps" is a location, and one can only imagine that the "her" of this poem has cracked her skull against that edge. It's important to note, now, that for such a short poem, Arnzen has set up two separate realities that are coexisting. The "I" has pushed the "she" down the stairs and has either killed her or done her serious injury. In a sense, these two realities collide:

breaks my waltzing daydream

So now, the "dance" has been defined as "waltzing," which is particular and formal, even down to the steps and how they are taken. So, again, this is a full idea, but one that not only builds on the poem that comes before, but is also redefined by it. This continues into the next line, where "waltzing daydream" is given the aural sound:

with its off-beat tempo

This is a specific type of sonic imagery. "Tempo" suggests a rhythm, but "off-beat" makes it irregular. Then again, this is one idea limited to one line, but it's facilitating the development of the poem as it stretches towards its (anti-climactic) conclusion:

and I hear another voice sing / as I stumble forward

Now, a wholly new element is intruding into the poem. We, as readers, can't possibly know whether the new voice is the woman that's been pushed down the stairs, or whether it's possibly a voice in the first person singular's head. Much of the poem, really, is about the interior of the "I." In total, the "her" only has a few lines all to herself. Basically, she gets pushed, and she smacks her head on the stairs. The rest is just a delusion of the "I."

Still, this poem couldn't exist if Williams had never written "The Red Wheelbarrow" and invented the Imagist movement, which has had a profound influence on American poetry. Arnzen's poem, like Williams', is actually a string of images and ideas that interconnects while moving down the page. The line breaks heighten this, and they also go a long way in creating a psychological sense of tension. Like "The Red Wheelbarrow," "The Fall Down the Stairs of the House of Usher" is really a singular moment in time, and if that is the organizational principle of the poem, there can be no moral resolution for the crime committed.

So there you go. Michael A. Arnzen, whether he knows or not, has written a poem in the shadow of "The Red Wheelbarrow" and all those other snappy little wonders Dr. Williams used to jot on his prescription pad, whiling away the moments between seeing patients.

*

This essay is an expansion of an analysis originally posted to Richard Ristow's weblog and no longer available online.

Rich Ristow is a Rhysling Award-winning poet whose work has appeared in the *Nebula Showcase*. His most recent book is, *Wood Life: A Poem*. His e-chapbook, *Four Murders*, was exclusively published by the Merchant's Keep web store. Also, he edited the anthology *Death In Common: Poems From Unlikely Victims*.

Original Introduction to the First Edition of *Gorelets: Unpleasant Poems* (Fairwood Press, 2003)

These poems—like all poems—were an experiment. What distinguishes these texts is the way they were written and the way they were intended to be read: on a portable handheld computer, or "PDA," like the popular Palm Pilot. Whenever the urge struck, the poet composed on a 3"x3" screen with a stylus.

Consequently, no poem here is longer than eleven lines and each of those lines contains no more than eight words, at best. Brevity and word economy was the rule. But if you study them, unique structures and patterns will emerge. The medium certainly shaped the message.

As did the genre. Gorelets are "horror" poems: a mode of writing which explores the "dark side" and muses over morbid themes like death, murder, disease, mutation, chaos, mutilation, the uncanny and all things outré. This is the genre I work in, mostly because I believe it is the most experimental popular genre. In it, one expects the unexpected, which requires the writer to break with convention at every turn.

Tapping into the popularity of the fiction genre, horror also brings a new audience to poetry. That was part of my goal: to get more readers in the digital age to take notice of poetry. When I began this project I realized that e-books were everywhere, but nowhere was poetry. And poetry just seemed to "fit" the screen better than long, eternally scrolling documents written for print rather than pixels.

Gorelets were like applets—tiny computer applications—only darker than the usual fare. I think these pieces hold up rather well considering each one fits on a screen the size of gauze bandage.

So read and bleed. They'll be quick jabs, but I hope nothing will clot the cut.

—Michael Arnzen, Halloween 2003

Bram Stoker Award Acceptance Speech for *The Goreletter*

Winner: "Superior Achievement in Alternative Forms" Category, 2003

17th Annual Bram Stoker Awards Ceremony
June 5th, 2004. Park Central Hotel, New York City

Wow. Thank you all so much. This is my second Stoker—I won the other one way back in 1994 for my first novel, *Grave Markings*—and I want to say thanks, HWA, for a very precious set of bookends.

Ever since I won that award a decade ago, I've kept a comic clipped out of the newspaper and taped by my desk to keep me humble. In it, a man in a suit sits on his sofa polishing a trophy and sipping a glass of wine. On the other side of the living room, a woman in a bathrobe and curlers holds a mop and says, "That's nice, dear, but it's still your turn to clean up the cat puke." The caption beneath reads: "When the real significance of an award hits home."

The glory doesn't last forever, but it sure does feel good right now. And I have a lot of people to thank for it. Above all, I want to thank my wife, Renate, who has always been there for me to talk to, run ideas past and simply spend time with. Believe it or not, we're celebrating our eleventh wedding anniversary tonight. And I want everyone here to know that she's actually cleaned up the cat puke for me many, many times just so I'd have a little extra time to write. *Frau, Ich liebe dich.* Happy anniversary—this award is for you.

I also want to thank my readers—particularly those who subscribe to my electronic newsletter, The Goreletter, which you are honoring with this award tonight. I'm proud to join the ranks of other e-letters that have won Stokers—Jobs in Hell and Dark Echo. I've tried to approach The Goreletter as a creative workspace rather than a rote announcement list and I think it's safe to assume that this trophy means I'm doing something right. God knows what that is, but it's gotta be something different. Because for all its confusion, that's all that this category "Alternative Forms" really means: something different. There is a rumor that this award category, "Alternative Forms," may not exist next year. And I can see why. I worry that it has become something of a dumping ground of the miscellaneous—a space for recommending "none of the above." After all, it's difficult to judge what's best when you're weighing, say, a film soundtrack against an Internet search engine or a newsletter or multimedia CD. But somehow we manage to award the best experiments with form time and again. This category may very well be odd, but it's also important. We are living in an era of alternative forms, and I would like to think that this category allows us to not only recognize that fact, but also remain actively engaged in our era. Ultimately, horror, too, is an alternative form in the literary marketplace. And for that reason, I am doubly honored to receive this award. Thank you all very much.

*

Postscript:

The Horror Writer's Association voted to eliminate the Alternative Forms category for the Bram Stoker Award in 2005.

PUBLISHING HISTORY

The original "Gorelets: Unpleasant Poems" book collected individual works that were distributed over the internet via www.gorelets.com, once per week from August 2001 to August 2002. Each poem was written on a rudimentary Handspring Visor handheld computer intended for an audience of other handhelds, and they were delivered directly through a variety of online posting mechanisms, including AvantGo. Concurrently, picture postcard versions featuring a poem with accompanying digital artwork went to patrons who generously supported the series with a donation.

In 2003, a print collection of the original 52 poems was published in a paperback edition (along with a 26 copy signed/limited lettered edition) by Fairwood Press (www.fairwoodpress.com).

The twenty-one poems in "Extra Unpleasantness" all originally appeared in The Goreletter or elsewhere on gorelets.com and were featured in an "Expanded Ebook Edition" of *Gorelets: Unpleasant Poems*, published by Double Dragon E-Books in 2003.

"Even More Unpleasantness" and the other sections of *The Gorelets Omnibus* are the kitchen sink for anything else. This book attempts to capture all the horror poetry that ever appeared (and in some cases disappeared) on the website at gorelets.com over the past decade, whether in print, audio, or animated form, but many of these poems also were reprinted elsewhere. Selected verse and essays (including material in the expanded hardcover edition, like the "Haikruelogy") have also been published in the following venues: *Byline, Cemetery Poets: Grave Offerings, Decompositions, Doppel-ganger, The Dream People, Dissections, The Eternal Night, Eye Contact, Hellnotes, Horror Writer's Association Newsletter, The Magazine of Bizarro Fiction, microcosms, Pittsburgh City Paper, SPWAO Newsletter, Star*Line, Wicked Hollow,* and *Wired News,* in addition to the Arnzen collections and chapbooks, *Chew, Freakcidents, 100 Jolts: Shockingly Short Stories, Proverbs For Monsters, Rigormarole: Zombie Poems,* and *Sportuary.*

Several poems from *Gorelets* were adapted to film and appear in the DVD, *Exquisite Corpse* (Jim Minton Design Group/Poeticollage, 2006).

Among the bonuses featured in the hardcover edition of this book, the parodic long poem, *Michael Arnzen Dying,* was originally published in collectible chapbook by Tachyon Publications in 2003.

The hardcover edition of *The Gorelets Omnibus* also includes a special "horror poetry writing workshop." Some of the "Instigation" prompts featured in that workshop were first syndicated in *Hellnotes newsletter* from 2002-2005, or also appeared on the early "premium" page of gorelets.com, "The Sickolodeon." Today, a complete ebook collection of "Instigation" is planned for separate availability on amazon.com, for those who don't have access to the hardcover *Omnibus.*

ABOUT THE AUTHOR

Over the past two decades, Michael Arnzen has won four Bram Stoker Awards for his avant horror fiction, his quirky dark poetry and his bizarro antics online at gorelets.com. His titles from Raw Dog Screaming Press include a novel (*Play Dead*), a collection of flash fiction (*100 Jolts: Shockingly Short Stories*), a CD of musically-enhanced readings (*Audiovile*) and, forthcoming, a scholarly study of dread in pop culture (*The Popular Uncanny*). When he's not writing, Arnzen wears the mask of professor of English at Seton Hill University, home of the country's only MFA degree in Writing Popular Fiction. Get gored again and again at gorelets.com or join his social network at michaelarnzen.com

www.ingramcontent.com/pod-product-compliance
Lightning Source LLC
LaVergne TN
LVHW011350080426
835511LV00005B/234